HOW TO
MAKE INFLUENTIAL DECISIONS
FOR SUPERIORITY

IAN COOMBE

First published 2018 by Independent Ink
PO Box 1638, Carindale
Queensland 4152 Australia
independentink.com.au

Copyright © 2018 Ian W. Coombe.

All rights reserved. Except as permitted under the *Australian Copyright Act 1968*, no part of this publication may be reproduced, stored in a retrieval system, or transmitted in any form or by any means, electronic, mechanical, photocopying, recording or otherwise, without prior written permission from the publisher. All enquiries should be made to the author.

 A catalogue record for this book is available from the National Library of Australia

978-0-6482663-3-4 (paperback)
978-0-6482663-8-9 (epub)
978-0-6482663-9-6 (kindle)
978-0-6482663-7-2 (audio)

Cover design by Alissa Dinallo
Edited by Elizabeth Turner Editoral Services
Internal design by Independent Ink
Typeset in 11/15 pt Times New Roman by Post Pre-press Group

WIKID POWER and SHIFT ME NOW are trademarks used by the author.

Disclaimer
Some names have been altered to keep the identities of some individuals private.

All the information, techniques, skills and concepts contained within this publication are of the nature of general comment only, and are not in any way recommended as individual advice. The intent is to offer a variety of information to provide a wider range of choices now and in the future, recognizing that we all have widely diverse circumstances and viewpoints. Should any reader choose to make use of the information contained herein, this is their decision, and the contributors (and their companies), authors and publishers do not assume any responsibilities whatsoever under any conditions or circumstances for any damages, libel or liabilities arising directly or indirectly from the contents of this publication. It is recommended that the reader obtain their own independent advice.

*I dedicate this book to
my mother and daughters
who asked the impossible-to-answer question
"Are you a spy?"
and to all those who encouraged me to tell all.*

*It is also dedicated to those of you with a
passion for knowledge and success
in whatever you are doing.
I hope this helps!*

ACKNOWLEDGMENTS

I acknowledge that my passion to solve problems drives me.

As I strive to articulate solutions and rationale in the simplest way, I find it vital and vitalizing to seek fresh eyes and perspectives to tackle my conclusions and explanations. For highlighting to me the numerous improvements I could make with my book, I am eternally thankful to my partner Donna, publisher Ann and editor Libby.

My time at Army Headquarters was made more enjoyable by having around me clever people with a sense of humour and passion for improvement. I thank my dear boss and mentor Ian Ahearn for the many "passionate discussions" and for his full support in all I achieved at G building and in my business. I also thank Mark, Peter and Richard (you know who you are) for the lateral thinking sessions discussing WIKID POWER.

Many great thinkers are mentioned in this book and I acknowledge their incredibly positive contributions to the theory and practice of decisions and success. They have helped me and millions of others enormously. May there be many more to stimulate our minds.

TABLE OF CONTENTS

Foreword	ix
WIKID Conception and Birth	**1**
It's Hard To Believe!	3
First Principles	5
"That's WIKID, Ian"	11
Beyond "TOP SECRET"	13
Valuable Information	15
WIKID POWER	**19**
Joining the Dots	23
Data	25
Information	29
Knowledge	33
Intelligence	35
Wisdom	39
Power	43
Superiority	**55**
Ages of Civilization	59
Environments	61
Success	65

Tips for Using WIKID POWER in Practice   **71**
  Cycling   75
  Good Judgement and Uncertainty   77
  Reason vs Emotion   81
  The Frontal Lobe   97
  Because and Therefore   101
  Asking Questions   103
  Finding Gold   115
  The Three Effs   119
  Converting From Human to Electronic – and Back   121
  Timing   125
  Priorities   133
  Behavior   141
  The Getting of Wisdom   153

From a Sneeze to World Domination   **155**
  Sneezing   157
  Broccoli   159
  Teenagers   161
  Stock Market Scams   163
  World Domination   165

What is the WIKID Value?   **171**
  Spies and Thieves   175
  The WIKID Punch Line   181
  Three Common Trip-ups   183
  My Three Vital Tips   185
  Your Personal Value   187

About the Author   191

FOREWORD

This book is in your hands because you have a passion for knowledge and success. If not, stop and hand it to someone who does – going further may be tedious if you lack a driving desire.

It is ironic that it took so long for me to decide to write a book on decision-making. Once committed, it only took six weeks to write. Converting much of my much-loved WIKID POWER presentation and adding real-life stories and examples of WIKID POWER from throughout my life was exciting. To some, this is self-indulgent. At times, it may appear I'm talking about unrelated issues. But the more times you travel through this book, the more you'll go from beginner to advanced and understand how to apply WIKID POWER and achieve success, personally or professionally. Some sections will be difficult or irrelevant – skip them until you are ready for them.

I love people with a passion to succeed and look forward to hearing your story.

Dan

WIKID
Conception and Birth

IT'S HARD TO BELIEVE!

My handover from my predecessor was simple: *"You're responsible for spending $30 million on software each year – and for policy."*

We then changed the combination to the safe and signed over the classified files. (I never understood why the SECRET files were colored salmon pink – not very macho.)

And then he left. Not only did he leave the building, but he left Army and moved to a small country farm on an island.

I was left with an office, an empty filing cabinet, an empty bookshelf and a safe filled with classified files.

Walter Burley Griffin created impressive plans for Canberra, using key geographic features as focal points for a triangular amphitheatre with a central man-made lake. Australian Army Headquarters is located at one of the three apexes which was devoted to the military; the other two to parliamentary and civic functions. One of the sides that crossed the lake came straight into the military apex and bisected the menagerie of buildings that formed Defence Headquarters. At the time, the buildings were named A to N and because Army was the largest component, it occupied the whole left side (buildings G-N) whilst the remainder of Defence shared the right side (buildings A-F). The two architecturally imposing buildings immediately on either side of the centre (buildings G & F) housed the offices of the key advisers in Army and Defence respectively. These two, courtyarded, four-story, square buildings were Australia's equivalent of the USA's Pentagon – but on a significantly reduced scale.

The office I now found myself in was on a middle floor of building G, within spitting distance of the Army's top General, the Scientific Adviser, Special Ops, the communications cell, finance and the Strategic Planning and Planning Directorates.

Being responsible for policies, I scoured the office for them but couldn't find any. I asked my colleagues where they were.

To my surprise, I was told that they weren't in writing. If someone wanted to know a policy, they would phone and I would be expected to think of a reply. I found it hard to believe that I was responsible for spending $30 million on software without a planned approach. I was shocked into action.

FIRST PRINCIPLES

Mapping the Army

I started working from first principles.

Spending the $30 million was a priority. If it wasn't spent in that financial year, the following financial year's budget would be cut – a bureaucratic idiosyncrasy based on the idea that if you didn't spend your entire budget, you were a poor budgeter or didn't need the money which would be better allocated to those areas that did need it.

I set about working out what software was needed. To do that, I needed to understand exactly what Army did. This would seem obvious to many, but Army is actually a very complex beast.

It quickly became clear that to support all of Army's operations with software, I needed to map all of Army's processes. This had never been done before.

The method I employed, Business Process Modelling (BPM) using IDEF0, of which I quickly became Army's expert, highlighted that what I considered the most critical process for Army, decision-making, was not supported by software.

Solving the Decision-Making Problem

I had learned about Artificial Intelligence (AI), computer programming, operational research (OR), Boolean logic and other rational problem-solving disciplines in my university studies. Experiments in physics and chemistry and my Army Officer training, including the Military Appreciation Process (MAP), a method of analysing a situation, producing options, deciding a course of action and preparing a plan, provided further foundations for the inculcation of my decision-making process. My mind was conditioned for decisions!

I spoke with senior academics and we established the University of New South Wales (UNSW) Group Decision Support System (GDSS) Research Group. We looked into elements which would affect decision-making: the environment, temperature, lighting, positioning, group size and technology. It was intriguing. What interested me most were two competing software applications – one using individual keyboards with a central screen, the other using screens for each participant. The geeks chose the former (they could touch type) whilst I chose the latter (I couldn't).

I went back to my office and began devising the development of a complete, self-contained group decision support system. I found the only distributer of the software I preferred, and we designed a portable system. Two metal cases contained cabling, ten notebook computers loaded with the software and a printer. It was almost a two-man lift per case!

Cunningly, I prepared all the proposal and justification paperwork and waited until the end of the financial year. This is the time when I knew there would be some people in Army Headquarters who hadn't spent their budget and were desperate to spend it before 30 June so that they wouldn't lose it the following year. All I had to do was to walk the corridors and chat with other Officers, asking how they were going with their budgets. When I struck someone with a huge shortfall – BINGO – I solved his problem and he solved mine!

The system had to be paid for and delivered by the end of the financial year. I simply gave the green light and two weeks later, we had our system. I was trained and ready to start trials.

It could be set up in a conference room with a projector and screen. Simple and neat.

A Decision-Making Capability

I started off doing simple meetings like strategic plans, business plans, project plans, budgets, system requirements, technical specifications and document development.

I developed various agendas for different uses, the instructions and taught others as facilitators. In essence, I was building a self-contained group decision-making capability, a new productivity addition to the traditional round-table conferences that introduced technology for the first time.

My boss would occasionally be asked for me to facilitate important meetings and at times, even though my job building the capability had already been done, I was seconded for these projects because my boss earned favours he could call in later. It usually raises eyebrows when I say I facilitated a crisis issue for Defence's top Admirals, the Strategic Plan for Army's Strategic Planning Directorate and the consensus allocation of Army's $10 billion budget (in a few hours!)!

I taught facilitators to go through this process in the agenda:
- Diverge: collect all the ideas
- Converge: amalgamate ideas into a manageable list
- Consensus: gain group cohesiveness about a decision
- Action: work the decision to deliver results

What's Knowledge?

The GDSS process required the contributions of the people with the expertise, information and knowledge needed to be in the room. Their input was critical in producing worthwhile decisions and outcomes. A good analogy is of an oil refinery taking the raw material and refining it into a useful product.

Working in the Information Systems Directorate, and being responsible for databases, I found I had reached a dilemma when I explained the transformation of their input: why are the words data, information and knowledge used interchangeably? Being pedantic with semantics, I set out to find the answer.

"Words Are Like Bullets"

In my early days in Army Headquarters, I found it took quite some effort to get to know the TLAs and FLAs – Three and Four Letter Acronyms used in the military – but also to learn to write in a way that would get things done.

A senior officer, who later became a boss, great friend, mentor and co-worker in my business, would say "words are like bullets". His message was to use them carefully, choosing the right ones with the right meaning for the right situation. So I gradually started shooting all the words at my office whiteboard.

information   data   knowledge

I knew there was a connection.

I also knew they related to decisions, so I added more bullets.

diverge   converge   consensus   action

I looked for the connection. I played with the words.

The gods were smiling on me.

The Connection Clue

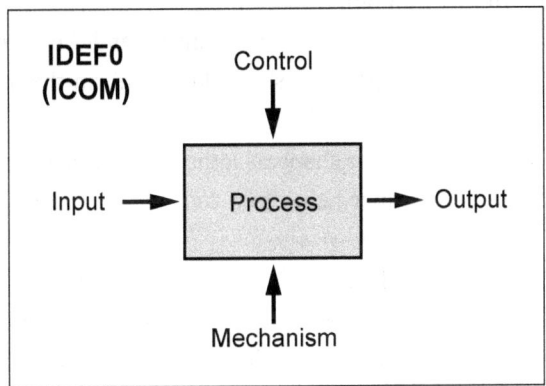

My work on software mapping and the GDSS not only led me down the path of decision-making, but also led me to BPM (Business Process Modelling) and IDEF0 (ICAM DEFinition for Function Modeling, where "ICAM" is an acronym for Integrated Computer Aided Manufacturing).

When explaining IDEF0 during facilitation sessions, it was simple: nouns and verbs. Nouns (arrows) are the "things" and verbs (boxes) are the "processes" that use the "things".

Inputs are processed into outputs by mechanisms with controls.

Example:
Bake a cake is the process (verb)
Inputs are the ingredients (nouns)
Controls are the temperature and time (nouns)
Mechanisms are oven and mixer (nouns)
Output is the cake (noun)
The output is often an input to another process (eg eat morning tea).

Break and Rebuild Until It Won't

I started building my model.

I took "things" (like data, information and knowledge) and tried to work out what "processes" could transform them into other "things" (outputs).

My model began taking shape as a theory of transformation.

In Physics, I remember being told *that you can't prove a theory right, you can only prove it wrong.*

Doing legal work, I remember being told that you just keep looking from different perspectives to find issues that can go wrong or break a contract and keep fixing it so it can't be broken.

With these in mind, I set about shooting my musings on the whiteboard in my office. I'd get to a point where I thought there was a gap, research and add more nouns and verbs.

I'd take regular breaks and, over the weeks, it began to take shape. Each time I researched an issue, I'd compare it to my model and see if it fitted; see if the model explained it, or not.

I kept to my mantra. *Find what's wrong – fix it. If it won't fix – tear it down and rebuild! Repeat.*

It increasingly took shape. I couldn't break it any more.

"THAT'S WIKID, IAN"

As I was running out of ways to break it – it had started to concrete itself into permanency – a colleague who was the go-to Information Warfare (IW) expert in Defence heard about my musings. He invited himself to a meeting in my office and we sat down together at my whiteboard. I rambled – in a structured way.

When I had finished, he looked up with a glint in his eye. "That's WIKID, Ian."

I struggled to understand. "Huh?" My father would have been proud of my elegant articulation of thoughts.

My colleague pointed it out to me and I have described it that way ever since.

BEYOND "TOP SECRET"

Although my colleague was quite fit, he was pleased that his long trip across the Defence Headquarters compound was worth it. He asked me to put together a "WIKID presentation" for his bosses.

That started the ball rolling. It has since been presented, among others, to:
- Admirals, Air Marshalls and Generals
- Australian, US, UK and other country authorities
- The highest Military Intelligence course in Australia as an opening keynote address, two years running
- A highly classified US Information Warfare course.

After giving a private WIKID POWER presentation to one particularly influential General, he went cold.

Stone cold.

I didn't want to interrupt his quite obviously serious thought, so I left him to make the first move.

"Ian," he started before drawing a breath. I had become used to him calling me by my first name rather than by rank and surname. Formality had been dispensed many years earlier, since we had quite a few dealings together. "I believe that the WIKID POWER framework you presented will give Australia a ten-year advantage over other nations." Having worked with other nations and seen their work and direction, I realized that he had grasped the impact and importance of WIKID POWER.

I braced respectfully. "Quite possibly, Sir." The loosened formalities only went one way!

"You see, you've clearly shown us how to gain advantage over any country, force or . . . or . . . anything really."

My eyes lit up. "Correct," I said quite humbly, happy that my presentation was clear enough and simple enough to be understood, and that it had impact. In a bureaucracy, like Defence, presentations were common. Boring presentations of little value were also common and were despised as time-wasters. I was reassured that my presentation was not boring and was of some value.

"I think I will need to classify it beyond TOP SECRET."

Oops. That was more value than I had hoped. I had to stop this from happening. If it did happen, there would only be a few who would be able to see it and the real value of WIKID POWER is if it is widely used.

There were three other reasons:
1. I wanted to use it as a basis for the Army Information Management Manual I was instigating
2. I had been approached by two university departments to write a PhD on it, and wanted to pursue that
3. I wasn't authorized beyond TOP SECRET and would be prevented from reading or working on my own material – how awkward!

It took a while after our meeting, but I eventually managed to convince him not to pursue that thought. He realised the classification would be more harm than help; we needed to get as many of our forces to learn it as possible, as the more of our people using it, the greater likelihood of superiority.

VALUABLE INFORMATION

The Cleaner Spy

While convincing the General not to classify WIKID POWER beyond TOP SECRET, I had to deal with a new problem.

Random Access Memory, computer data storage known as RAM, was being stolen from the computers in G building. RAM was expensive at the time and the computers in Army Headquarters had loads of it. The computer would be physically opened and any additional RAM would be removed, leaving only the basic RAM. Without video surveillance, we could only hypothesize how it was happening. Our favorite idea was that the cleaners were taking the RAM after hours.

This situation led me to consider an interesting scenario – A Spy in Army Headquarters.

It went like this.

- When asked if people believe spies exist, everyone says they do
- When asked if they think that other countries are spying on Australia, everyone thinks they are
- When asked if they think spies may have infiltrated Army Headquarters, most think they have
- When asked if a cleaner could be a spy, most agree it would be relatively easy.

Assuming some cleaners, who operate after usual work hours, could be spies looking for valuable information the next question is: where would they look? Maybe the huge metal safe, with the combination lock on the front, in the corner of an office? Assuming again that they are trained, it would be a simple matter to crack the safe and look inside.

Amongst all the material in there, the next dilemma for them would be to isolate the high-value material from the lesser-value material. Fortunately, our military assists spies by using unusually salmon-colored pink folders for SECRET material.

If we wanted to make life more difficult for spies, I would simply put the highly-classified material on my now overflowing bookshelves in plain folders. Good luck to any spy that could find the good stuff in there!

Access to information of value is important to consider.

A "Spy" Disappears

I made a habit of walking the corridors in Army Headquarters regularly, chatting with other Officers about their work. I obtained information of value and saved myself an enormous amount of work by knowing where the useful information was, to access it for leverage into my own work.

On one particular occasion, I wanted to obtain access to information I was authorized to have, but did not have clearance to use the access mechanism. I was walking the corridor and mentioned this irony when the person said that they could help me. They managed to easily use the system they were not authorized to use.

This person had become part of the furniture over the years, as someone representing an allied nation. They had even told me that they were expected to be there another few years.

Unfortunately, the access they displayed appeared to be more than an aberration or luck. They had systematically worked over time to gain access. I mentioned this to an appropriate person and coincidentally, the representative wasn't there the next day – or ever again. It was never mentioned. It appears a "spy" had disappeared because they sought access to valuable information.

So, where is the value in information? Power and control.

It becomes clear that information is transformed so that its value increases to deliver power and ultimately control.

WIKID POWER

Acrostics are a favorite tool of mine. When facilitating decision-making meetings, I noticed that successful strategic plans had 5 +/- 2 goals, and business structures had a span of control, the number of subordinates being managed at a level, of 5 +/- 2. The reason for this is also the reason that most memorable speeches have 5 +/- 2 points, and phone numbers used to have 5 +/- 2 digits, and are now broken down into smaller groups of three or four digits.

The reason is ease of memory. Let's face it, we only have so much we can cram in. The easier it is to remember something, the more likely we will. And if we remember something, we consider it important. If it's important, we have an attachment to, or ownership of, it. Establishing a sense of ownership is key.

You'll notice that another example of this magic size is in social settings, groups of more than 7 often split into smaller groups of people because of the human inability to process larger group interactions.

People with the most amazing memories either have a freakish mind or a memory retention tool to help such as mnemonic pegs. I decided to introduce relevant acrostics as mnemonic pegs. Ideally, the acrostic reflects the focus e.g. HEART for a heart charity values: Hope, Equality, Awareness, Respect, Transparency. Thankfully, there are not many words that are longer than seven letters, hence acrostics are well suited to lists of 5 +/- 2.

The result was stunning, both with strategic plans and WIKID POWER. One General I had presented to recited the WIKID acrostic a year after I presented it to him!

WIKID POWER are two related and interwoven acrostics that should help you remember how to make influential decisions.

JOINING THE DOTS

My draft PhD thesis began:

> *Wise corporate executives teach their protégés that information is power. National security organizations turn data into intelligence. Philosophical gurus are proclaimed to be wise and enlightened because of their knowledge. Communications and Information Systems professionals interchangeably use data and information. Dictionaries tell us that knowledge is information. How is it all interrelated?*

These various states of information are usually considered equivalent:

information = power = data = intelligence = wisdom = knowledge

However, if we give them order and remove the equals signs, we begin showing how they are all related.

Data is transformed into
Information which is transformed into
Knowledge which is transformed into
Intelligence which is transformed into
Wisdom which is transformed into
Power which is transformed into . . .

That's how it ended up on my office whiteboard.

In BPM/IDEF0 terms, WIKID represents inputs and outputs (nouns), while POWER represents the processes (verbs) that transform them.

How each element is transformed is the other piece to the WIKID POWER theory.

DATA

Data is the first and most basic element of WIKID POWER.

Data is observed symbols, values or signals.

Unfortunately, if you went to a dictionary for their definition, you would find yourself in a circular definition. Variously, dictionaries confuse matters by using words such as information, thing, decision, facts, measurements, observations and descriptions to describe *data*. However, the only key words here are observations and decision. *Data* needs to be observed to assist the decision process.

Example:

32, 2911, 826, Smith, Mitchell, Brown

At this stage, these are only observed symbols that convey no specific meaning to you.

Data is observed and collected. It can be observed with any of the human senses and also be observed via sensors such as microphones, electromagnetic devices and other devices.

Data, and the WIKID POWER process, relate to electronic, physical and human media.

Two Tons of Ballistic Calculation Equipment

As a Troop Commander in the Army, I was delighted to be responsible for a rare battlefield capability: Sound Ranging. Five microphones were placed about 1 km apart in a line parallel to the Divisional frontline. For every microphone, two parallel cables – one for redundancy - were laid back to the command post behind the microphones – which kept the linesmen very fit indeed laying, tying off and pulling in about 30km of cable with each move. Each microphone cable was attached to a pen recorder, similar to earthquake detectors, in the plotting station. They would twitch if a loud sound passed over the microphone, and this would be recorded on fast scrolling paper. Since it was not practical to have the paper scrolling continuously, listening posts were deployed in front of the microphones. Their job was to immediately inform the plotting station to turn on the recorders when they heard the primary noise from enemy artillery. The time difference between each microphone's detection was plotted and trigonometry used to calculate the position on the battlefield from where the enemy artillery was fired. The recordings also showed the secondary sound of the exploding shell, and the time difference approximately represented the time of flight (with a slight adjustment for the time sound takes from the two locations), and therefore range, of the enemy artillery. Variations in the pen-recording patterns also indicated the type of weapon fired, caliber and other characteristics. Calculations needed to consider wind, air temperature and echoes or reflections from geographic features such as valleys. A plotting board was used to process the *data* from the pens to determine locations and ranges were worked out using a mechanical computer. All this equipment was in the back of a two-ton truck used as a command post. From the command post, counter-battery fire (CBF) was able to be directed and the sound-ranging equipment used to adjust our own fire onto the target with accuracy.

I only had command of the Sound Ranging Troop for one year before the equipment was retired from operational service. In that year, the sound ranging calculation was converted by my Troop Sergeant Major and me into a computer program we wrote on a brand new handheld HP41cv calculator. We then swapped the truck for a Land Rover since we didn't need all the calculating equipment anymore! This example demonstrates all three possible states of data:

electronic, physical and human.

INFORMATION

> *Information is data that is recognized in context to convey meaning.*

Your brain processes the *data* streaming in from your optic nerves, sensitive fingertips, vibrating ears, tingling tastebuds and twitching nostrils. Yet, just as *data* can be in different states, so too can *information*. *Data* is stored in fields in a database, which define their context and relationships. Objects such as bits of paper, wood and metal are arranged to form a library. And food ingredients (*data*) are arranged in context to form a dish.

To recognize *data* into a context, the relationships need to be identified and understood.

Example:

Brown is 32 years old and lives at 826 Smith St, Mitchell, 2911

The previous data is now information, because it has been identified and recognized in an understandable context – in this case, an address.

Lightening Doesn't Need to Strike

When I joined the Army, I entered the Royal Military College, Duntroon to study for an Electrical Engineering Degree. In the second year, we were required to undergo work experience as part of the curriculum. As a result, four weeks of my holidays were consumed in a 9–5 job working for the national telecommunications organization, Post Master General (PMG), a precursor to Telstra. At least I enjoyed the evenings and weekends! My project was to see what I could do about testing telephone lines after a storm.

The problem was this. For every phone line – known as a pair because it comprises two wires – a signal booster was required every 1.82 km. This distance was used because the drums of wire were that long and it was easy to put a booster at each join. The booster was a coil of wire in resin, about the size of a large human eye. Every time there was an electrical storm, customers would phone, if they could, and complain about the static noise on their line. The noise was because one or more boosters had been blown out. The blow outs were not necessarily from a direct strike, but more often because of what is known as induction whereby a nearby electrical current, such as the lightening bolt, sets up a magnetic field which can in turn produce another electrical current – as is the case with electromagnets. When static was reported, a technician would then need to physically check *every* booster, known as an inductor, from the exchange to the terminal (customer). This was time-consuming and expensive.

I had test signals sent down the line from both directions. The *data* from the test was then entered into a program I wrote on a programmable handheld calculator. By recognizing the context of the *data*, useful *information* was produced.

To take it further, this test result became the calculator's *knowledge*, which was compared against other *knowledge* I had stored in the calculator. This produced the technical *intelligence* of how many boosters had been blown and precisely where they were. The foremen would then *wisely* send out technicians to replace only the blown boosters. This saved PMG time and money and gave the supervisors more *power* to deploy their technicians to other tasks.

This story is not only a practical example of the transformation of *data* into *information*, but also a terrific example, to come back to later, of the entire WIKID POWER process that is unfolding for you.

KNOWLEDGE

Knowledge is information that has been experienced.

Experience includes assimilation. For a person, this usually means it has been committed to memory. *Knowledge* includes experience (implicit *knowledge*) as well as that which can be articulated (explicit *knowledge*). *Knowledge* is a part of an object, such as a computer or a person, when its meaning is understood. Electronically, *data* is stored with appropriate relationships to be considered *information*, which may then be accessed by a computer program and used to help determine some resulting decision. This stored *information* would be considered electronic *knowledge*.

Example:

The information about Brown only became your knowledge when you experienced it by reading, assimilating and understanding it.

Information about Brown is now your knowledge.

Thesaurus and Dictionary

Just prior to my posting to Army Headquarters, I was sponsored to do a higher degree, a prerequisite for my new job with software. I was fortunate to have an allowance for books as part of the sponsorship. Two of my favorite purchases were the hardcover deluxe editions of the latest dictionary and thesaurus.

At Army Headquarters, I was fortunate to have two other Officers who obtained perverse pleasure testing theories. We were known as TOTS – an FLA acrostic for Thinking Outside The Square. One day, when brainstorming my ideas, one of them questioned me about *information* and *knowledge* and challenged me that they may be the same. I looked around my office and handed him my prized dictionary.

"Have I given you *information* or *knowledge*?"

This has become one of my favorite examples because it is an "aha!" moment for many. The moment of realization that *information* can be possessed through a gift from someone else, but *knowledge* is only gained through the personal work of experiencing and assimilating that *information*.

One of my other colleagues believed his role was to be a *knowledge* repository for his organization and kept everything he learned to himself rather than use it for greater purposes. In other words he was like a thesaurus he didn't want opened. For a smart guy, he lacked *intelligence!*

Unfortunately, many Knowledge Management (KM) proponents also tend to stop at *knowledge*. Generally, there is agreement about the transformation from *data* to *information* to *knowledge*. However, *knowledge* is able to be transformed further. The key is to understand the purpose and wonder why one is observing *data*, recognizing it and experiencing it as *knowledge* through assimilation.

INTELLIGENCE

> *Intelligence is knowledge assessed through wonder.*

Many people incorrectly think that when I use the word *intelligence*, I am referring to cleverness, as in Intelligence Quotient (IQ). What I am really referring to is *intelligence* as in the expression military intelligence or business intelligence.

Goals are the key to understanding *intelligence*, in this sense.

From the outset, before *data* is observed and collected, there must be a purpose or desired outcome for the transformations that are to occur. The desired goal drives *intelligence*.

Intelligence is only gleaned by wondering if it meets the goal, and adding and assessing *knowledge* until it does.

Intelligence requires an understanding of the implications of *knowledge*. *Intelligence* is deduced after several pieces of *knowledge* are assessed together – each with their own level of uncertainty. As relevant and useful *knowledge* is added, uncertainty decreases. Additional *knowledge* is continually added and assessed until the level of uncertainty is acceptable for the *intelligence* sought. *Intelligence* provides options for decisions and action.

Example:

> When collecting the data on Brown, the observer had the goal of finding cases that might require social assistance. When assessing the previous knowledge about Brown, the assessor wondered if other knowledge was required before making a decision about the need for assistance. When combined with the knowledge that 826 Smith Street is the address of a homeless shelter, the resulting intelligence is that Brown is homeless.
>
> If this level of uncertainty is unacceptable – he may be the caretaker – then more knowledge is added until the level of uncertainty is acceptable and further data is processed until the intelligence about Brown meets the initial goal.

Military Intelligence

History is replete with examples of poor *intelligence* analysis. It is also replete with stunning examples of impressive *intelligence*. Modern TV shows involving crime forensics and sci-fi wars highlight the WIKID POWER process, especially the transformation of *data* through to *intelligence*.

When I was the Brigade's Artillery Intelligence Officer, *data* was continuously observed and transformed into *information* we could process into our human *knowledge* or our computer *knowledge*. Analysts always assigned a level of certainty or confidence to each piece of *knowledge*. Sometimes the situation mandated a quick decision based on less-than-desirable certainty, resulting in incomplete or uncertain *intelligence*. Such is the nature of the battlefield. Should more certainty have been required, the first step may have been to send reconnaissance teams out to observe and gather more *knowledge* – these teams having a specific goal and purpose to ensure the resulting *intelligence* delivered the desired level of confidence.

Knowledge needs to be continually added until the *intelligence* is produced with an acceptable level of confidence.

Risk Analysis of the Largest Australian Entity

One of my more memorable decision facilitation sessions was immediately after leaving Army. My facilitation experience had become known outside Defence and I had been headhunted to facilitate a risk analysis for the largest organization in Australia – the Department of Health and Family Services. All the key people were there, about 20 in all. By mid-morning, we had already achieved the objective of obtaining a list of risks to the organization. The participants were delighted that this was more than they had hoped as the outcome of the facilitation. However, I had been contracted for the whole day and had not finished with them to my satisfaction.

I held up an object and asked them its color. They were unanimous but I disagreed with them. Then I turned it around so that they could see it from my perspective – it had a different color on the reverse side.

Perspective is vital.

Before lunch, I asked them to list more risks from different perspectives – from that of the Department, from doctors, administration staff, patients, and more. The list grew. They were incredulous at the result.

After lunch, I took a different perspective on perspectives. I asked them to list risks according to the perspectives indicated by Dr Edward De Bono's six thinking hats, one for each distinct direction in which the brain can be challenged: Managing, Information, Emotions, Discernment, Optimistic response and Creativity.

The feedback I received at the end of the day, apart from everyone being mentally exhausted from thinking, was that they now had a more thorough list of risks than they had ever hoped. It was a resource that allowed them to build a stronger business for many years to come.

Intelligence requires wondering about whether the available *knowledge* is sufficient to help move towards a goal, and wonder works best when different perspectives are used.

WISDOM

Wisdom results when intelligence is applied, through decisions, to an opportunity.

For many people, *intelligence* is enough, but if a desired goal is the aim, *intelligence* is merely a prerequisite and a milestone to achieving that goal. *Wisdom* is the decision to apply *intelligence* to the opportunity that will help achieve the goal. *Wisdom* requires an understanding of the principles for future action. *Intelligence* is of no practical use unless applied by making a decision for action, thus *wisdom*.

Example:

Since Brown is possibly homeless, it would indeed be wise to have a social worker talk with him in case he is homeless and needs assistance.

Once the *intelligence*, that Brown may be homeless, is applied to a social worker opportunity, *wisdom* prevailed.

Global Financial Crisis

The worst financial crisis since the 1930s Great Depression hit in 2008. Many large financial institutions collapsed and the financial market was threatened. After stunning increases, the US housing market slumped in 2006. Desperation for refinancing and other factors caused financial markets to plummet from July 2007. On 9 August 2007, a run of withdrawals from three major hedge funds were terminated because of lack of cash. Markets fell 50% over the next 15 months. I watched as many lost much of their wealth because the *intelligence* of a freefall was plain to see, but the *wisdom* to take action wasn't.

Four Months and Four Plane Rides

Within months of joining the Army, I was off for a few days during the Easter break in what the Army called "adventurous training" where some element of risk was required. The two activities I selected were abseiling and parachuting. I loved trying new things and I had done neither of these. It was an amazing thrill to run full speed over a cliff and down the cliff wall face-first ("carabiner run down" was what they called it) on my first day abseiling, but of more interest was parachuting.

These were the days prior to tandem jumps and rectangular air rammed chutes that enable you to flare and touch down lightly on your toes. We used old circular WWII chutes that you could barely steer. We were told the fall was like jumping off the third floor of a building, so we practiced. We learned how to jump out of the plane (Cessna), steer, bend the knees, turn into the wind to slow prior to landing, fall and roll. Then came time to go up in the plane. Loving the thrill, I sat on the floor at the opening where the right door used to be. My reserve chute was on my chest and I covered it, as trained, with my arms to prevent it accidentally opening and pulling me out of the plane and onto the tail. As we taxied down the grass landing strip, and gently lifted off the ground, I marveled at the view of the terrain below me. The lush rural setting was littered with green pastures divided by wood and wire fences and sprinkled with cattle, all getting increasingly smaller. Pushing my memory, I recalled other scenes like this on TV. (*data – information – knowledge*) Then an amazing piece of *knowledge* popped into the front of my mind and with stunning clarity, I deduced the following "this is my first ever plane ride" (*intelligence*). I was staggered that it hadn't occurred to me until I was up in the plane, and chuckled at how stupid I was not to realize earlier!

I was the first to jump. Despite this being my first plane ride, it made no difference to my goal to parachute. Despite the *intelligence* this was my first plane ride, I also concluded the *intelligence* that I wanted to jump and now knew how. I was set on my decision to take this opportunity to jump (*wisdom*). With excitement and a racing heart, I waited until the instructor directed the pilot to slow the engine and, with a nod from the instructor, I unhesitatingly reached out with my left hand to grab the strut and then stepped out with my right foot onto a step about the size of a pencil case. Simultaneously swinging my left foot over to stand it on the tyre, I brought my right hand over to grab the strut near my left hand. My right foot now swung in mid-air. I looked over to the instructor to get the nod to jump, and the thought that crossed my mind was "I hope I don't fall!"

In hindsight, my mind was bringing in other pieces of *knowledge* I had about heights. However, my overriding desire and driving goal was to jump – so the decision to jump was easy, and I did. I had exercised *wisdom* and *power* over a fear.

As a self-indulgent postscript to the story, I jumped three times that weekend, landing 50m, 5m and 20m from the mark – amazing for my first jumps with an old round WWII chute. Four months later, I took my fourth plane ride of my life – a commercial flight home – and landed during a fierce electrical storm. The landing was rough. I was understandably hesitant going up in the next plane again after that. It wasn't until my fourth plane ride that I actually landed in a plane – four months after I had first taken-off.

POWER

> *Power occurs when wisdom participates influentially in an environment.*

Wisdom to take action does not necessarily result in action.

There are many examples when someone will say they should do something, but never actually do it. I'm sure you can think of some! Decisions and actions do not equate to *power* unless they actually influence the situation.

Example:

Brown's standard of living improved once the social worker visited him and utilized social programs to help him find a job and home.

Power results when *wisdom* is used to participate with influence in an environment. That's WIKID POWER!

My First Assignment

An atmosphere of excitement and anticipation buzzed in the small, clinical classroom where the first class in my Master's degree was to take place. The lecturer walked in and gave an impressive introduction. It went something like this: You are now postgrads. No longer undergrads. We don't want you to regurgitate textbooks in your assignments – we expect you to use your minds and to put forward new ways of thinking in your assignments.

I loved this new approach. To be given not only permission but encouragement to unleash a previously restrained and constrained mind, rather than mindlessly accepting and following like sheep.

And then came the assignment. Capacity Planning – how to plan IT for the future.

As you read this, it will be difficult to picture a world where the Internet did not exist in its modern form. The source of all *information* was kept in libraries. Remembering my time management techniques from my undergrad degree, I immediately visited the library after class. There, to my delight, the lecturer had placed two references on reserve and I quickly signed them out – a chapter of a book and an article. My bibliography was looking sparse. After taking notes, and finding nothing else in the library, I asked the librarian if she could find other sources for me outside the library and to my delight there was a periodical titled *Capacity Planning*. BINGO. It was an international journal and to my amazement there was only one known subscriber in Australia. It was the Australian Bureau of Statistics (ABS) and they were about a ten-minute drive away. BINGO and JACKPOT.

I managed to sweet-talk my way into the ABS staff library, and my steps grew faster as I saw the aisle with journals. There on the shelves was my Holy Grail – two cardboard journal boxes full of issues of *Capacity Planning*. It took no time at all to find several articles on the exact topic, with varying views to those expressed in the reserve selections. The assignment was compiled with a large bibliography and comparing various viewpoints before concluding my own opinion. (*data – information – knowledge – intelligence – wisdom*) I handed in the assignment (*power*) and visualized the High Distinction I'd get, having been resourceful to find other material and doing exactly as instructed by using my own thinking rather than regurgitating. Not one other person in the class knew of the extra material and all the others used only the reserve material in the library.

The results returned. All the others received Distinctions and I received . . . a bare Pass. What? I quickly learned to give the lecturers what they really expect, and not to point out extra issues they were unaware of.

Power to influence doesn't always translate into success!

A Desire To Take Action

Power is about taking action. Many people want to take action but are not driven to take action. Some say that there is a big difference between a wish and a goal: a goal is a wish with a plan, timeline and desire to get it done.

As a military leader, I thought that discipline and motivation drove action. Then I heard a motivational speaker say that you can't motivate anybody. You can inspire and coach, but you need to help them find their own motivation. As an adviser to business leaders, I felt it important to understand this better.

I distinctly remember incidents with all of my favorite long-standing clients asking for help in improving various aspects of their businesses. With a sense of excitement that they were initiating progress, I would show them simple solutions to their issues. Every one of them have, at various times, not actioned the simple solutions to the problems. It bewildered me that they evidently weren't motivated to significantly improve their businesses.

It's said that there are only two motivators: fear and greed. Fear motivates through the consequences of losing, or not having, something such as love, respect or community belonging. Greed motivates because of the benefits of gaining something. I found this idea useful.

Many I advised were struck by the simplicity of cause and effect. Motivators cause a resultant effect, and if the motivations are used well, the effect is success. I highlighted the fear and greed issues with my clients – sometimes this worked, other times there appeared to be no impact whatsoever. I don't think they wanted improvement strongly enough to take action, whatever the consequences. Maybe they were scared of trying something new, maybe they were comfortable with the old way, or maybe the consequences weren't significant to them.

My faith in thinking that fear and greed were the only two motivators wavered. I now believe that what stirs someone into action and success is not necessarily discipline, fear or greed but <u>desire</u>.

Maslow's Hierarchy of Needs

Maslow's Hierarchy of Needs is a theory in motivational psychology first proposed in 1943, and was taught as one of the first leadership lessons in officer school. The theory parallels many other developmental theories such as the stages of growth. It describes the patterns of five levels of motivations and desires that humans move through.

The five levels increase from basic needs to more sophisticated needs with each level ideally being fulfilled before the next level. The five levels are, from the bottom basic level:

1. Physiological – breathing, food, water, sex, sleep, excretion, homeostasis
2. Safety – security of body, employment, resources, morality, family, health, property
3. Love and Belonging – friendship, family, sexual intimacy,
4. Esteem – self-esteem, confidence, achievement, respect of others, respect by others
5. Self Actualization – morality, creativity, spontaneity, problem solving, lack of prejudice, acceptance of facts.

Maslow coined the term "Metamotivation" to describe the motivation of people who go beyond the scope of the basic needs and strive for constant betterment.

Metamotivation, and the increasing five levels of desire and need, helped me understand my clients' behavior better and why some didn't necessarily implement the solutions that would've brought success.

The Magic Ladder of Success
Napoleon Hill, considered one of the most inspirational and influential authors of all time on success, listed eight basic motivating forces as the starting point of all human achievement:
1. The urge towards self-preservation
2. The desire for sexual contact
3. The desire for financial gain
4. The desire for life after death
5. The desire for fame; to possess power
6. The desire for love (distinct from a desire for sex)
7. The desire for revenge (a characteristic of undeveloped minds)
8. The desire to indulge in egotism

This list is a better breakdown than simply fear and greed.

In a military sense, Hill's motivators for success might be self-preservation, power and egotism (to live to be the best) although the altruistic motivation is to protect a nation which would be classified as the first motivator, self-preservation.

In a business sense, Hill's motivators might be finances, fame, power and egotism (to be better than your competitors) although it might simply be an internal drive for *power* through success.

In a personal sense, Hill's motivators might be any of the eight.

Someone who may only want to have great *knowledge* might be motivated to fame, *power* and egotism.

Those who seem to have no motivation may instead be motivated primarily by self-preservation, keeping things simple and uncomplicated to the degree where they can handle the issues they deal with routinely and do not feel overwhelmed.

No matter which situation, Hill's eight motivators appear to cover most situations.

DNA Of Success

As I continued to look into motivators, I attended a seminar by Jack Zufelt, titled "The DNA of Success". He defined a "Success Attitude" being required for a "conquering force" and lists four key ingredients for success:
- Core Desire – a case of heart over mind; passion
- Direction – a plan to reach your goals & success
- Proper Action – deciding and doing the right things
- Persistence – overcoming obstacles

He demonstrated an emphatically compelling equation that, if followed, guaranteed success. Whilst the mathematical relationships are not explained, he produces a simple equation (with the acrostic SADD PAP) that he claims we follow – intentionally or not – for success:

$$\text{Success Attitude} = (\text{core Desires} + \text{Direction}) \times \text{Proper Action} + \text{Persistence}$$

Having been through the rigours of developing and testing my WIKID POWER model, I tried to find flaws in Zufelt's model, but it seemed to fit every experience I could recall.

Central to the equation is Core Desire. Zufelt claims that whatever you desire most, you will achieve. If you desire something else even more, it will force its way to your attention instead. He suggests you rate desire out of 100, where 100 is a Core Desire, and nothing will get in your way of achieving it.

Life In Half A Second
I attended a seminar about influential people, with a rather charismatic and entertaining speaker, Matthew Michalewicz, author of *Life in Half a Second*. He claims there are five doors to success. The five doors reinforce Jack Zufelt's equation, although they differ in perspective. What is uncanny, is that one of the doors is Desire. Like Zufelt, he explains that desire is a measure of how much you want something. He claims desire guides every decision and action. Without desire, it will be easy to be distracted by other things that compete for your attention, time, and effort. The desire that is the strongest is most likely to get all your attention and action, and is therefore most likely to succeed.

Career Advice
Conversely, if you attempt something with a weak desire, it is easier to become distracted and fail. This concept parallels the sage career advice to avoid jobs where you have no passion: If you love what you do, you'll never work a day in your life.

Working in alignment with your desires makes the effort easy. Desire drives you to:
- observe useful *data*
- transform *data* into *information*
- transform *information* into experienced *knowledge*
- transform *knowledge* into *intelligent* conclusions
- transform *intelligence* into *wise* decisions

Desire drives your motivation to convert decisions into **action**.
A stronger desire increases the **influence** and *power* of action.
Power that attains a desired goal produces **success**.

POWER Acrostic

You have read the *information* I have provided, and therefore have the *knowledge* that there is more to WIKID. Did you wonder what it was, look to find and observe other *data* that would reveal the acrostic? If so, I congratulate you on transforming the *data* into *information, knowledge* and *intelligence*. If you worked out what the POWER acrostic was, then you have not only demonstrated *wisdom* and *power* – but you have gone further. You have succeeded.

Power, the transformation from *Wisdom*, is not only the output (noun/thing) of the WIKID process, but it is also the acrostic for: Participation, Opportunity, Wonder, Experience and Recognition.

The WIKID and POWER acrostics dovetail.

Did you see the double acrostic and how they interrelate?

Data	+	**Recognition**	=	Information
Information	+	**Experience**	=	Knowledge
Knowledge	+	**Wonder**	=	Intelligence
Intelligence	+	**Opportunity**	=	Wisdom
Wisdom	+	**Participation**	=	Power
Power				
WIKID Power represents the nouns/things.				
POWER represents the processes of transformation.				

Recognize
You need to recognize the context of *data* to transform it into useful *information*.

Experience
Information must be experienced (electronically, physically or humanly) for it to be transformed into *knowledge*.

Wonder
To deduce conclusions and *intelligence* from *knowledge*, you need to wonder how it contributes to achieving your goal. Will your *knowledge* give you confidence in your *intelligence*?

Opportunity
Intelligence sits idle and unattended unless there is a core desire that motivates you to decide to seize the opportunity to take action – *wisdom*. A core desire propels you towards a committed decision to take action, whereas a weak desire has a chance of being ignored in favour of other, more appealing desires.

Participate
Having made a *wise* decision about what action to take, power is only demonstrated when action is taken and it influences the environment. Not all action though is successful.

Revisiting the Sound Ranging Troop
When I introduced *data*, I told of my time as Commander of the now-defunct Sound Ranging Troop. It highlighted not only the three states of *data* (human, electronic and physical) but I also pointed out that it was an example of the entire WIKID POWER transformation. Here's how it works.

Advanced Post	*Data* (human ears)
Sound via cable to plotters	*Data* (electronic signals)
Pen Recordings	*Data* (physical marks)
Analyst reading recordings	*Information* & *Knowledge*
Plotting to get enemy location	*Intelligence*
Counter Battery Fire	*Wisdom*
Silence the enemy artillery	*Power* & Success

Now that's WIKID POWER! But let's move onto superiority and success!

Superiority

What is success all about? Success is the attainment of control or superiority over a situation or environment.

I prefer to call it superiority. There are solid reasons to call it superiority rather than control or success:
1. Control has a flavor of ongoing manipulation, which some consider unethical, although not all situations of superiority are unethical or require ongoing manipulation.
2. Success is considered an outcome of a plan but not all situations of superiority are planned.
3. Superiority is a well-accepted term that is used in many environments.

Superiority is about mastery over yourself, an adversary, a situation or an environment.

AGES OF CIVILIZATION

Throughout history, mastery has been the key to superiority in every age. As the earth turns, our view of it changes and new technologies change the way we do things.

Gone are the agrarian, bronze, industrial and nuclear ages. We are now engulfed in the information age, whipped into a frenzy by a pervasive use of the Internet, where too much *information* is barely enough.

The first step of mastery comes in the identification and use of the leveraging technology. Superiority results when the efficiencies and effect of your technology of that age outweigh that of others'. If you use technology better than others, you experience superiority. Consider the superiority of farmers over hunter-gatherers, civilizations that used metal tools over those that used stone, Henry Ford's assembly line, the Cold War standoff between USA and USSR, or the leveraged success of Internet retail over bricks and mortar shops.

As we have progressed through the ages, the amount of stored *information* has increased dramatically. Yet, until recently, this *information* was stored in libraries – the technology being books – so only the elite who could visit libraries became *knowledgeable* and *wise*. Now, almost anyone can access the stored *information*.

According to some sources, a human's brain capacity devoted

to memory is only 200 megabytes and if a human's entire life (words, sounds, images) was recorded, it would consume only 6 gigabytes. The world produces more *data* storage now than it can humanly produce or remember, and since we have amazing access to an immense store of *data* in our databases and on the Internet, it becomes even more vital to efficiently process it for our needs, by filtering the *data* through selective observation, recognition and experience – transforming *data* to *information* to *knowledge*. To further transform that into *intelligence* and *wisdom* and ultimately *power* and *superiority*, we need a technology to make those processes more efficient.

Information Technology (IT) is the technology expected to deliver that efficiency in the Information Age.

As I worked in G building in Army Headquarters, that was exactly my goal – to ensure the Army efficiently mastered IT by transforming, *data* through *information*, *knowledge*, *intelligence* and on to *wisdom*, *power* and *superiority*.

ENVIRONMENTS

In the world when I first presented WIKID POWER, we sought superiority in various environments.

Military Environments

In the military, three environments existed:

>Sea, Land and Air.

Warfare was conducted in each environment:

>Sea Warfare, Land Warfare and Air Warfare.

Power was exercised through warfare in each environment:

>Sea Power, Land Power and Air Power.

Combatants each sought to be superior and control their environment over their adversary by the use of their power:

>Sea Superiority, Land Superiority and Air Superiority.

The terminology was clear, accepted and used in these three environments with consistency.

Shortly after my first presentations of WIKID POWER, there were some interesting uses of technology to gain advantage over their adversary in a fourth environment. I was privy to *knowledge* of an operation where key command posts of a particular force, and therefore their entire command and control system, were rendered inoperative through the strategic inclusion of certain software in some of their recently purchased technology. This clever technique brought the conflict to a very abrupt conclusion and saved many lives that could have otherwise been lost fighting a war in one of the three traditional environments.

It was a win without the loss of lives, and a win for Information Warfare: an operation I described as fought in a new Information Environment. It was a win in the Information Age through Information Superiority via the efficient use of Information Technology.

When compared across environments, the terminology was consistent, and I argued that the military needed to add this new Information Environment to its doctrine. And we needed a General to head it up.

Information Warfare was a new concept in Defence Headquarters and I was developing a framework for it. They were exciting times! My push to induct Army's first Chief Information Officer (CIO) was successful. Defence followed soon after.

National Environments

I looked more expansively at the following five National Environments that were used to discuss national security:
Military (as above)
Social
Economic
Political
Geographic

Other environments being considered for inclusion were:
Industry
Infrastructure
Science

I was advocating to also include Information

The effective use of WIKID POWER requires a consistent terminology to be applied to each environment. To this end, WIKID POWER would require the following expressions be considered and used for National Power:

Military	Environment	Warfare	Power	Superiority
Social	Environment	Warfare	Power	Superiority
Economic	Environment	Warfare	Power	Superiority
Political	Environment	Warfare	Power	Superiority
Geographic	Environment	Warfare	Power	Superiority
Industrial	Environment	Warfare	Power	Superiority
Infrastructure	Environment	Warfare	Power	Superiority
Scientific	Environment	Warfare	Power	Superiority
Information	Environment	Warfare	Power	Superiority

In reality, WIKID POWER is applicable in any environment such as, life stages, vocation or even hobbies. The focus is superiority and success in any environment.

SUCCESS

In the military context, success is the achievement of a mission. In common usage, it translates to achievement of a goal. Let me reiterate that *power* is not enough. Going through the WIKID POWER process is not enough.

In practice, you set a goal and aim to succeed by attaining it. Success is simply gaining control of oneself, a situation or an environment. It has been suggested to me that control is unethical. While I understand there are contexts where this may be true, there are other contexts, perspectives and environments. On the contrary, control is what everyone desires. Control over a situation is what determines success. Psychologically, it is well known that anxiety is a feeling of being out of control and many stressful situations and psychological conditions result from a fear of, a threat of, or actually being out of control. Conversely, we are happiest when we feel in control. To gain control is to achieve success and happiness.

- Do students merely want to attend and participate at university or to control their results and earn a degree?
- Do job seekers merely want to apply for jobs or to actually control the selection process and get jobs?
- Do entrepreneurs only want to have a business? Or do they want to control their business and their part of a market?

- Do parents merely want to interact with their children? Or do they want to control them to the degree that they teach them values, fun and how to grow into independent young adults?
- Do children want to control their parents? Absolutely! And many do! Because they have learned that by controlling a parent, they get what they want, their desire is fulfilled and they have achieved success.

How does WIKID POWER operate in practice? WIKID POWER is about solving problems! Gaining control. Here's two quick stories to illustrate.

Time Management Techniques for Essays
Army Officer Cadets who studied Engineering were generally considered to be mathematically and regimentally minded when compared to those who studied for an Arts degree. However, when it came to essays, the Arts students won hands down. Having studied Engineering, I was accordingly apprehensive as the Military History unit of study began, and I discovered the assessment was based on four essays. I was motivated to join other senior Cadets in the bar rather than languish in my room late every night for a week poring over an essay four times. I used my logical engineering mind to solve the problem of how to write a satisfactory 1500 word essay in the shortest possible time – and get to the bar! Here's how it went:
- I write about 10 words per line.
- There are about 10 lines per paragraph.
- Therefore, there are about 100 words per paragraph.
- Therefore, in a 1500 word essay, there's 15 paragraphs.
- Each paragraph is an idea. Therefore 15 ideas.
- Essays have an introduction, body and conclusion.

AND

- A body should contain no more than three key points.
- Therefore,
    1. Introduction
        a. Topic   1 para: 100 words
        b. Definitions   1 para: 100 words
        c. Aim   1 para: 100 words
    2. Body
        a. Point 1
            i. Ideas   1 para: 100 words
            ii. Discussion   1 para: 100 words
            iii. Conclusion 1 para: 100 words
        b. Point 2
            i. Ideas   1 para: 100 words
            ii. Discussion   1 para: 100 words
            iii. Conclusion 1 para: 100 words
        c. Point 3
            i. Ideas   1 para: 100 words
            ii. Discussion   1 para: 100 words
            iii. Conclusion 1 para: 100 words
    3. Conclusion
        a. Summarize points   1 para: 100 words
        b. Concluding opinion   1 para: 100 words
        c. Next Step?   1 para: 100 words
- Further,
    1. It's relatively easy to write any paragraph of only 100 words without research.

2. DO NOT waste time on reading or taking notes – which often leads to bias and information overload.
3. Write the outline (paragraph headings) first.
4. Fill each paragraph, flowing as if speaking.
5. When finished, and only then, look at references.
6. Find enough references for an impressive bibliography and note section.

Using this method, I completed each of the four essays within hours and was at the bar before dinner. The feedback was that my essays flowed, they were easy to read, and my references were impressive! The results exceeded my goals. I topped three of the four essays and won the military history prize.

The method is simply about time and project management as well as capacity planning. I wince every time I see someone research and take notes furiously before planning what they write.

I have shown this method to several others since, from primary school to university. They all have applied it with similar success. They too have achieved superiority over their environment.

The relevance of this story is the application of the WIKID POWER process
- to have a goal (write an essay AND go to the bar early)
- observe *data* (length of essay and words in a paragraph)
- make *information* my knowledge
- wonder whether the *knowledge* helps attain my goal
- deduce *intelligence* by combining relevant knowledge
- take an opportunity to make a *wise* decision how to act
- take action and participate in the essay environment
- influential *power* produced success and *superiority*

Three Force Multipliers
Success in the military was also taught, unsurprisingly. Military training inculcated the doctrine of force multipliers – aspects that leverage your true *power* and can lead to success by making your force more impacting.

When I was taught this at the Royal Military College, the environment was the battlefield. When consulting to business leaders, the same force multipliers applied to their situation – in the market. Every CEO I've discussed this with has found ways to apply the three force multipliers to achieve greater success. And, as I look back on some of my favorite parental situations, force multipliers applied there also!

The doctrine varies at times and may include extra multipliers such as weather, terrain, technology and time but they all can be reduced to the three key multipliers that I was taught.

1. *Firepower* is the first. It relates to sheer weight or numbers. Those with more firepower have a force multiplier that can greatly influence the situation. The range of a weapon, the number of troops, the speed of a car, the best lawyer, more experience, cash in bank.
2. *Manoeuvre* is the ability to be agile and flexible to adapt to a changing situation. To react to a stock market correction, adjust tactics on the sports field when behind, change routes if a road or airport is blocked, have mobile forces outflank large slow-moving troops, have a backup plan, decide to go out if you burn the dinner, comfort a child when they hurt themselves, outwit a teenager.
3. *Morale* is what Napoleon Hill calls his first law of success, the Master mind, or *esprit de corps*. An ability for a team to have values that put the group ahead of the individual, to think as a team and to act as a team or family, parents working together when challenged by children, children ganging up on parents. A mindset where one steps in to support another almost without thinking.

The best examples of this are sport teams and military units, where it is not only how well trained they are (firepower) but also their agility (manoeuvre) and teamwork (morale). When I was young, I was in a hockey team. We weren't the top division, but we all enjoyed each other's company and were passionate about having fun and working with each other. One particular incident I remember was when the play made a slight switch and instantly I moved into a different position on the field whilst my teammate moved alternatively. We didn't even look at each other but seemed to know exactly what each other was thinking. With such teamwork, it is hardly surprising we won the grand final that year.

The relevance of force multipliers is the application of the WIKID POWER process to:
- have a goal (be a superior force – a goal builds morale)
- observe *data* (situational awareness)
- turn *information* into knowledge (capabilities/firepower)
- wonder whether the *knowledge* helped attain my goal
- deduce *intelligence* by combining knowledge (manoeuvre)
- take an opportunity to make a *wise* decision on how to act
- take action and participate in the environment
- use force multipliers to gain *power*, success and *superiority*

So, what have I learned when applying WIKID POWER?

Do I have three key tips or essentials to help ensure *superiority*? Yes.

But I want you to consider and practice the following tips first.

Tips for Using WIKID POWER in Practice

When working your way through the WIKID POWER transformation, it is useful to have a few tricks up your sleeve to make your efforts easier.

CYCLING

At various times, people will contest whether something is *data, information, knowledge, intelligence* or *wisdom*. The truth is, the same piece can be all of them! Let me give you some examples.

What Goes Up Must Come Down

- Computers send electrical signals – which is *data* – to the screen to light up various pixels. The signals become light *information*.
- Pixels are *data* until they form an image on the screen, such as a letter of the alphabet. The pixels then become *information*.
- Letters of the alphabet are *data* until they are recognized in context as words. The words become *information*.
- Words are meaningless unless recognized in context as sentences. The sentences become *information*.

This is an example of cycling through the WIKID POWER transformations until the correct level is reached. The transformations go up the WIKID POWER levels and, at various moments, are then cycled back in again at a lower level, only to rise through the transformations again.

When you wonder whether a piece you have is *data*, *information*, *knowledge* or *intelligence* – there's a good chance that you have them all at various times and stages.

Adding Wisdom and Power to the Cycling

To the astute reader, *wisdom* can also be cycled back in as *knowledge* when determining *intelligence* and *wisdom* – such as using feedback to adjust a plan.

Even *power* can be cycled back in. Some actions that are taken to influence a situation can result in the creation of new *knowledge*. As an example, the listening posts of the Sound Ranging Troop observe *power* being exercised on the battlefield and feed that back in as *data* which is transformed through as *information*, *knowledge* and *intelligence*.

As you work your way through the WIKID POWER process, you will repeatedly have to put one transformation back into the process at a different level. Keep cycling as often as you need. This requires good judgement.

GOOD JUDGEMENT AND UNCERTAINTY

Good judgement and uncertainty go hand in hand.

"In war, everything is uncertain" is attributed to the nineteenth-century Prussian General Helmuth von Moltke. He wrote, "No plan of operations extends with certainty beyond the first encounter with the enemy's main strength," which is now known by the more succinct expression "no plan survives contact with the enemy." Every situation is different and is therefore uncertain in outcome. Continually collecting *data* to reduce uncertainty runs the risk of analysis by paralysis. With paralysis, no decision is made, which can have dire consequences. In some circumstances, there is the luxury of time to collect more *data* and reduce uncertainty, but in others, when bullets are flying, or the stock market is crashing, or casualties need to be triaged, a decision needs to be made before it's too late to make any decision. Good leaders display confidence in their decisions to ensure trust, commitment and morale of the team – without it failure is often the result rather than superiority. As is so often stated, "a good decision in time is better than a perfect one late". We cannot remove all uncertainty and judgement is the key to know when to call it.

The use of WIKID POWER of course also involves good judgement, which will only improve as you become more accomplished at practicing it.

Judgement is especially important in the transformation of *knowledge* into *intelligence* – and of course in determining what additional *knowledge* you need before you can make a superior decision.

Incredible research into judgement and uncertainty has been the life-long dedication of Philip Tetlock, who put together a team of super-forecasters in his *Good Judgement Project (GJP)* to overwhelmingly win a tournament sponsored by the US *Intelligence Advanced Research Projects Activity (IARPA)* looking into how to improve forecasts of global situations. In his book *Super-Forecasting*, Tetlock says super-forecasters "beat competitors by forecasting more accurately". His process for super-forecasting echoes the WIKID POWER process of determining the goal, collecting various *data*, transforming it into useful *knowledge*, wondering about what *intelligence* can be deduced, and taking the opportunities to make *wise* decisions that result in superior forecasts. Rinse and repeat often.

What he has discovered is that it doesn't matter how smart or educated someone is, it is more the attitude and approach to problem-solving that separates the super-forecasters from the others. Further, this can be learned. WIKID POWER and super-forecasting are in lock-step.

Part of the solution to super-forecasting is breaking difficult questions into easier ones. An example is the classic question by Enrico Fermi – a central figure in the development of the atomic bomb. "How many piano tuners are there in Chicago?" To solve this impossible question required the solving of smaller easier questions:

- How many pianos are there in Chicago?
- How often do they need to be tuned?
- How long does it take to tune a piano?
- How many hours does a piano tuner work?

And the first question can be further broken down into:
- How many people live in Chicago?
- What proportion play the piano?
- How many pianos service the piano players?

Without the Internet or any references to look up, he guessed the answers to these smaller questions and calculated the result which was later shown to be highly accurate. This is a skill that needs to be developed to fully benefit from the WIKID POWER process – the ability to identify and collect smaller pieces of *data* that will help solve bigger problems. The inability to do this is what will stop many people from making superior decisions.

Another two areas where the lack of good judgement sabotages the likelihood of superiority is with the development of *intelligence* and with the decision to take an opportunity for action.

Many people gain the *knowledge* about a particular issue, only to progress further down the WIKID POWER process without gathering other *knowledge* that would produce better *intelligence*. With poor *intelligence*, the outcome is unlikely to be superiority. Some people stop collecting *data* too soon and others keep collecting too long.

Yet even with superb *intelligence*, the next speed bump where people stop the WIKID POWER process is applying the *wisdom* of a decision into action in the environment. Far too often, people know the wise action to take, yet fail to follow through. Without action, superiority in any environment is impossible. For some, the hurdle is emotional, and they find it difficult to apply reason.

REASON vs EMOTION

Realizing the connection between the practice of the WIKID POWER transformation process and superiority was emotional for me. Emotion has another important part to play in WIKID POWER.

WIKID POWER is a rational transformation. Logical. Reasoned.

There were times throughout life that I came across some utterly bewildering decisions. Emotional. Illogical. Irrational. Unreasonable.

For a time, I concluded that WIKID POWER couldn't explain these decisions and that the WIKID POWER process was only useful in an environment of reason and logic. I even toyed with the idea that maybe I'd have to develop another decision-making process to run parallel to WIKID POWER for irrational decision-making.

Eventually, it became clear. The process remained the same. If you find yourself dealing with an irrational situation, you still go through the WIKID POWER process, but add as much *knowledge* as you can to the process – *knowledge* about dealing with irrational situations. There is no second path. The path simply becomes more complex, and probably much longer! Much more cycling will certainly be required, and you may not find success as often, but the more experience and *knowledge* you gain, the closer success will be.

In trying to understand emotional decisions better, I researched.

Visceral Factors

Psychologist George Freud Loewenstein, a Professor in the Social and Decision Sciences Department at Carnegie Mellon University, has researched "visceral factors" such as a sales technique of invoking a sense of urgency by emphasizing that the deal may not last forever and you might miss out. His conclusion was that the heat of the emotion always precedes, and often supersedes, the cool rationality of time, reason and deliberation.

Emotion always precedes reason.

This mirrors the truism most sales people know that people buy emotionally and then justify with logic. The emotional outcome becomes the focus and logic disappears.

Not all emotions focus on similar issues or seek similar outcomes. For instance, when:

Upset	negative issues are the focus and placating outcomes sought;
Lonely	isolating issues are the focus and empathizing listeners sought;
Sad	victim issues are the focus and uplifting outcomes sought (but more prone to impulsive risk-taking);
Happy	progressive issues are the focus and advancement outcomes sought (but prone to ignore data analysis); and
Fearful	risk issues are the focus and precautions sought (yet prone to ignore facts).

So how much influence does emotion play in decision-making?

Mood as Information

In the 1970s and 1980s, psychologists Norbert Schwarz and Gerald Clore ran a series of experiments to determine how much emotions influenced decisions. They repeatedly found that people asked themselves "how do I feel about it?" before making a decision. If they were in a good mood, a positive decision occurred because it felt right. A bad mood produced negative decisions because it felt wrong. They called this phenomenon "Mood as Information" because the feeling was interpreted as credible *information* that needs to be considered in the decision-making process, even if it is contrary to the hard facts.

Manuscript Feedback
An example of how emotions can be infused into the decision-making process is when I recall showing my draft manuscripts for this book. At the time, I was also conducting new workshops for businesses along similar lines to my presentations to the military intelligence community. I received feedback that the second half, tackling the infrastructure required for *superiority*, was a tad complicated. I was taken aback – the military soaked it up with glee! I also got similar feedback about the second half of my book – again, tackling the infrastructure required for *superiority*. To put it bluntly, I was quite miffed. I had spent ages drafting that part of the book. It is what the military loved because it could give them an edge, and it is also a key part of my full WIKID POWER model. This felt like a personal issue – one I seriously wanted to ignore and push on regardless.

Nevertheless, within a day of receiving 175 words of feedback on my manuscript, I managed to conclude my reaction was "Mood as Information" and was taking on too much priority. I promptly sat down and cut out the complicated half and adjusted the rest. The feedback from other authors was genuinely credible *information*, my feelings were not! *Intelligence* deduced, *wisdom* decided and action taken.

Cognitive Bias

Psychological bias, or cognitive bias, is when some *information* is interpreted with preconceptions, thus giving flawed *knowledge* or leading to flawed *intelligence* and poor decisions. Such a situation will not lead to *wise* decisions or to sufficient *power* that is required for *superiority*.

The concept was first introduced in the 1970s by psychologists Daniel Kahneman, Paul Slovic, and Amos Tversky. They determined that decisions or actions that are made in an illogical way can be described as cognitive bias.

Cognitive bias is the opposite of common sense and clear, measured judgment. It can lead to missed opportunities, poor decision-making and is not likely to result in *superiority*.

There are some commonly quoted cognitive biases:
- Confirmation bias
- Anchoring
- Halo
- Overconfidence
- Gambler's Fallacy
- Fundamental Attribution Error

This section describes some of the cognitive biases, although a look through a more complete list would be well worth the effort. In all cases where cognitive bias may be present, gaining a second, unbiased opinion should help you make a better decision.

Confirmation Bias

The Military Appreciation Process (MAP) is driven into every Army Officer. The idea is to keep collecting *information* through reconnaissance (*data* collection) until you have enough *knowledge* to understand a situation (*intelligence*) and make a plan (*wisdom*).

As officers become proficient, this skill becomes easier and second nature. Some are prone to assuming they intuitively understand a situation and make plans based on false assumptions. It was often an instructor's delight to lull a student into false assumptions and unworkable plans that ended up failing disastrously. I found myself in learning opportunities a few times during my training.

Instead of appreciating (as in the military appreciation process) the situation, students often "situated the appreciation" by assuming they knew what was happening, and drove the appreciation process in the wrong direction.

Police investigations use the expression confirmation bias where the investigator thinks they know what happened and filters evidence to confirm their theory. This is a natural human cognitive tendency to find and collect information that supports your position – regardless whether it is wrong – while disproportionately giving other options less consideration. Care must be taken to avoid this error of inductive reasoning and stopping the WIKID POWER process too soon.

You are probably aware of people who have been wrongly blamed for something because of confirmation bias. Discrimination and bigotry are examples.

A study shows that confirmation bias is common when viewing statistics. People often look for *data* in statistics to support their position, and it is quite common for the distortion to occur through the simple changing of a word. People have a tendency to infer *information* that supports their existing beliefs, even when the statistics support an opposing view. It is critical to avoid confirmation bias when making statistics-based decisions.

A similar bias is known as availability heuristic, where people overestimate the importance of certain available *information*. For example, a person might argue that smoking is not unhealthy because they heard of a heavy smoker who lived a long life.

Survivorship bias is also similar; it's where surviving examples cause a situation to be misinterpreted. We might think that being an entrepreneur is easy because we only hear of the successes. Another, similar bias is the ostrich effect of sticking one's head in the sand and ignoring key *information*.

Anchoring
Anchoring bias is similar to confirmation bias in that a single piece of information is anchored as a sacrosanct and vital key for a decision. It is akin to jumping to conclusions based on first impressions. All other input is dismissed or adjusted away from the anchor. This severely limits the ability to consider the impact and consequences of new *data*.

One subset of anchoring is egocentric anchoring, where people assign their own experiences, contexts and knowledge to others. In other words, people tend to believe that others know, like and feel how they do. An inability to see issues from other perspectives can be catastrophic.

Here's an example where anchoring could've aided a situation to go terribly wrong. Early in my career, as the most junior of officers, I was responsible for the transport of an entire artillery regiment – hundreds of vehicles. Every week, the transport Sergeants and Corporals were required to send me all sorts of reports. Before the days of computers and printers, this was a laborious task, especially since much of the *information*, such as registration numbers, was repeated. As an efficiency nut, I designed a single report encompassing them all and gathered the supervisors to explain the quicker system. I wanted it to me by noon on a Wednesday. One Corporal said they couldn't do that and I immediately thought he was testing the newbie. I asked, "Why not?" and he claimed he couldn't read or write. I was stunned. I didn't know anyone that couldn't and thought he was kidding me. I asked how he passed his promotion exams and he said he had a trick where he had his wife read from the manuals into a tape recorder, a trademark technique that he was known for. We organized lessons and he progressed much faster, but his wife lost her expertise at military instruction!

Anchoring often happens when under pressure, especially time. To avoid anchoring, reflect on the value of pausing and gathering more information before jumping to conclusions. I'm glad I did not act on my first instinct with my Corporal.

Similar to anchoring is "recency" where the latest *information* is seen to have more influence. A good example of this is the inclination of some people to listen to the latest person to sway their mind and backflip decisions eventuate as a result.

Tunnel vision may also be considered similar.

Over-Confidence Bias

This occurs when a person overestimates their abilities, possibly on the basis of past experience or sometimes because of a lack of self-awareness due to limited honest feedback. It can happen especially when too much faith is placed in their own *knowledge* and opinions. They may also have an overinflated belief about the value of their contribution to a decision. This can sometimes be combined with anchoring, or acting on hunches, because of an unrealistic view of their own decision-making ability.

A research study found that entrepreneurs are more likely to have overconfidence bias than the general population. They can fail to identify limits to their *knowledge*, so they perceive less risk. As we know, not all succeed.

Early in my career, my boss told me he avoided dishonest sycophants, or yes-men, so that decisions weren't based on an unrealistic ability due to a swollen head. I joked with him that I wasn't a yes-man – if he said "no", I'd say "no" too!

Halo
This is where the perception one has of a person, company, product, brand, place etc. taints the assessment of any new and related *information*. For instance, if someone performs well in a particular area, the perception may be that they will automatically perform well in all areas. Or if one product is recalled, everything about that entity will be negative.

This is similar to overconfidence bias. It is also similar to bandwagon effect (also known as "groupthink") where people tend to lean towards a commonly held view.

Related is stereotyping and pigeon-holing, where the attributes of one are assigned based on the perceived norm for a category. This is often the case with discrimination against certain groups of people.

Yet another example is salience, where we tend to focus on the most easily recognizable features of something such as when you think about dying, you might worry about being killed by a shark, as opposed to what is statistically more likely, such as dying in your sleep.

Also related is blind-spot bias, where people tend to notice issues with others more than they notice issues with themselves. Of course, this isn't something that relates to us, is it?

Fundamental Attribution Error
This common bias occurs when something goes wrong. Instead of objectively looking at cause and effect, processes, or anything else, there is a tendency to immediately blame others.

You can see this often in politics. There are also some personalities which tend to put other people down so that they themselves look better. For example, you may be more likely to consider the other driver a worse driver than you if you have an accident where they are at fault. In reality, it could be because of many reasons such as bad weather, a mechanical fault, another driver caused them to take evasive action, etc.

Closely related is actor-observed bias, where blame is placed on external events; it is the opposite of fundamental attribution error. For example, if a car accident was your fault, you're more likely to blame the brakes or the wet road than your driving ability.

This is also related to selective perception bias, such as when you may tend to see more infractions of the rules by your opposing sports team.

Whilst not quite correlated, I tend to also think of pro-innovation bias here, when an entrepreneur or inventor tends to overvalue usefulness and undervalue limitations. When it doesn't deliver the results, actor-observer bias can take over. This was a common situation when I was responsible for Army's software and people would often propose a new solution fresh on the market.

Sunk Cost Fallacy

This is the situation where the investment is considered too great for a change of direction and this heavily influences decisions to stay the course. Also related to this is choice supportive bias, where you tend to favour your choices regardless of success. A good example is the choice of a pet or appliance.

Strongly determined people who stop at nothing to succeed sometimes succumb to this. The sayings "fail early and fail fast" and "cut your losses" reflect this bias. Also, the sayings "Don't throw good money after bad" and "a triumph of hope over experience" demonstrate that the concept of staying too long is well-known.

Whilst not directly related to sunk cost fallacy, the following biases may, in some situations, also have a similar impact: risk-aversion bias, loss aversion, conservatism bias (preference for prior evidence over new evidence) or zero-risk bias (avoiding new ideas with a possibility of not succeeding). For example, people were slow to accept that the Earth was round because they maintained an earlier understanding that the planet was flat and were reluctant to take on a new concept. A favorite humorous comment I've heard about this is that the flat earth people eventually came around.

Gambler's Fallacy
The gambler's fallacy happens when you expect past events to influence future events. A typical example is seen in betting games. If a coin is tossed and gets tails six consecutive times, you might expect a higher likelihood that you'll toss heads the seventh time when in reality, the odds don't change from one toss to the next: 50%. As is often the case, the longer the run of luck (or bad luck), the greater the belief that the chances of a change improve.

When going through WIKID POWER, you will have collected the *data* about the coin tosses, but be careful to not discard the *information* that the odds don't change with each toss. In business, a pattern of wins (or losses) doesn't necessarily mean a change is imminent.

A way to avoid gambler's fallacy is to avoid looking at the *information* chronologically and to instead look at it from many different perspectives.

A similar bias is known as hot hand fallacy (winning streaks) and clustering illusion, which is the tendency to see patterns in random events. This is also known as apophenia, the tendency to perceive a connection or meaningful pattern between unrelated or random things (such as objects or ideas). A common example is seeing faces in toast, grass, tiles, etc.

Another similar bias is outcome bias, where a decision is judged based on the outcome rather than how the decision was made. For instance, a gambling win doesn't mean it was good decision to place the bet.

How Con-Artists Use Cognitive Biases

For a scam to work, a con-artist needs to encourage us to abandon our well-reasoned decision-making skills and instead make subjective decisions that, in objective hindsight, were obviously flawed. A very well-honed understanding of decision-making is required for a scam to work or be thwarted.

Cognitive bias makes confidence tricksters' scams work. Maria Konnikova explains in her book *The Confidence Game* how psychology is used in scams and how we fall for it every time by having our cognitive biases exploited. Grifters rely on us abandoning good judgement and to ignore warning signs by leveraging various cognitive and emotional biases.

The eight steps to a scam are:

1. The put-up — identifying a mark susceptible to cognitive bias
2. The play — bait a victim through emotional trust
3. The rope — emotional pitch to lower defences and hook the victim
4. The tale — "too good to be true" to "I deserve this"
5. The convincer — give away wins that prove a bias that things will work out
6. The breakdown — a loss tests commitment & hooks the victim more
7. The send and touch — further investment from the victim & final fleecing
8. The blow-off and the fix — ensuring the scam continues

For a scam to work, French & Raven claimed, in their much-cited 1959 work *Bases of Social Power*, that there are five bases – the more a grifter can employ during the rope, the better. They are:

1. Reward   belief you will gain reward
2. Coerce   belief you can be punished
3. Legitimate   actual basis of trusted authority
4. Referent   affiliation with a trusted entity
5. Expert   subject mastery

Diligent use of WIKID POWER, especially in the treatment of *knowledge* to produce well-reasoned *intelligence* should also result in *wisdom* to identify and avoid scams – especially that you are now armed with this *knowledge*.

International Buy Out

When I was selling a part of my business to a multinational from New York, my antenna was up. I was looking for a solution that would solve my cash-flow issue after a major client defaulted on payment, and was easily identifiable as a mark. I had received a recommendation from a reputable business organization about an American firm looking to establish a foothold in our country. All five bases of social power were active to lower my defences, and the tale I told myself was that there may be some initial pain but it would work out in the end and that all my hard work deserved a reward.

Negotiations started and I believed I was winning. A reasonable price was agreed to, and I would not only salvage my position but would make a reasonable return for my efforts. Then reality hit: 20% was upfront and 80% after a year. It hurt but it sounded reasonable. I will be paid a wage for the year (a very good wage) and the 20% upfront was significant enough to break even and leave me without debt. I had already set my expectations of a good outcome. This test of my commitment made me more determined to achieve my initial expectation. As the year rolled by, I invested more of my time and effort (but thankfully not money) making the deal work. On the anniversary, they moved in and changed the locks and I saw no final payment. They were untouchable, in another country.

Knowledge of the five bases of social power and the eight steps of a scam may have helped me at the time better identify what was happening and I may have been able to negotiate better terms to not be scammed of such a large final payment. However, I had considered the possibility of a scam and thus ensured the 20% was enough to break even and ensured I was left in the black. A good example of the WIKID POWER process saving me financially. The American firm had knowledge of my desire to sell, and used that well to achieve their outcome – another good example of WIKID POWER. Since we both achieved what we wanted, we both achieved superiority – sadly, I was hoping for more superiority than I achieved!

State-Dependent Decisions

State-dependent decision-making is where decisions are made according to a particular situation. These decisions are not necessarily those that would be made under normal conditions, but are dependent on the current conditions.

There is much theory written about state-dependent decision-making and it often results in mathematics and probabilities. Without getting into the technicalities, it is sufficient to say that there are times that optimal decisions might only be made for a current situation, yet these decisions would not be made under ordinary circumstances. For example, many people can relate to the decisions they make to buy souvenirs they would otherwise not look at, simply because of the state of excitement during travels. Others can relate to purchasing specials at trade shows or in supermarkets because at the time, it looks like a bargain too good to miss. In a more serious situation, a hostage might make decisions that would not otherwise be made.

A Bad Time to Sell a House

After my first daughter was born, I was eager to settle into a home rather than continue to live in rental properties. I made a list of criteria to help the process then started perusing the newspaper adverts (in the era before the Internet) for houses which might satisfy my criteria. I unwittingly drew on my experiences to produce *knowledge* that I kept accumulating to produce the *intelligence* in the form of criteria for my perfect home.

I found an incredibly interesting house in an ideal location, within walking distance to the capital city's CBD, its most extensive park, its lake and my work. A quick investigation also revealed that it was the classic investment opportunity of the worst house in the best street, and the seller was the executor to an estate and was being urged by the beneficiaries to quickly sell all property and distribute the cash before real estate prices slumped further. The elderly executor lived in a rural community several hours' drive away.

The auction was midweek instead of the usual weekend, with about ten other properties, in the auctioneer's premises in the city rather than onsite. I was not prepared for an auction, nor fond of them, but I decided to attend to get a feel for the market. There were about six bidders in the auction room but only two bids in total, and none for the property I liked. All houses were passed in. The market slump was dramatically reinforced

Having experienced much more *data* through this exercise and converted it through to *intelligence* I thought it was *wise* to make an offer then and there, at the conclusion of proceedings. I made a ridiculously and insultingly low offer and, to my surprise, the executor accepted. Not only was that *power,* it was *superiority*.

It was serendipitous state-based decision-making for me because I would not have otherwise made such an offer, and the unfortunate state-based decision-making for the executor who would not have otherwise sold for that price.

State, or context, is clearly important.

THE FRONTAL LOBE

Through cycling, *knowledge* often is converted from *power* – lessons learned through experiences (successful and unsuccessful) of taking action. Parents, teachers, coaches, counsellors and mentors know this well. They pass on their *knowledge* to help others succeed.

An Old Head On Young Shoulders

Assistance to others grows in sophistication from teaching babies, to toddlers, teens and adults. As people go through life, they experience millions of WIKID POWER transformations, some deliberate and prolonged over time, and some intuitive or innate, taking only nanoseconds. These experiences all aggregate and accumulate as the years roll by. The more action that is taken (*power*) the more is learned through the outcome (success and *superiority* – or not).

An older person generally has much *knowledge* that could assist younger people. This truism is exemplified through the age-old saying "You can't put an old head on young shoulders." In essence, you can't *give* a person experience. What makes this frustrating is that, with a positive attitude and desire to learn, an inexperienced person can often learn from others without needing to experience something. As another of my favorite sayings goes, "A clever person learns from their mistakes. An even smarter person learns from others' mistakes."

Much of a person's *knowledge* depends on their attitude to learning from their experiences. Some see failed attempts as negative whilst others see them as positive – an opportunity to learn. Hill saw learning from failure as a Law of Success. The frontal lobe is the part of the brain that processes much of our experiences and helps our understanding of the consequences of decisions and actions. This understanding of consequences helps our judgment.

Judgment and Consequences

The frontal lobe is one of the four major lobes in the brain of mammals. Science has determined the *intelligence* that it contains most of the dopamine-sensitive neurons in the cerebral cortex. The dopamine system is associated with reward, attention, short-term memory tasks, planning, and motivation. Hence, it is responsible for judgment and consequences.

Depending on how well developed it may be, the frontal lobe can recognize future consequences resulting from current actions, the choice between good and bad, the comparison of better and best, the override and suppression of unacceptable responses, and the determination of similarities and differences. The frontal lobe is constantly cycling through the WIKID POWER process, and using memories of experiences as *knowledge* to help the transformations.

Memories

Frontal lobes also play an important part in retaining longer term memories which are not task-based. These are often memories associated with emotions. An undeveloped frontal lobe may not process this well.

It usually takes about 25 years to fully develop frontal lobes in humans, but can be earlier or later, depending on the person's environment and attitude to learning from experiences. A person can develop the ability of their frontal lobe through practicing rational thought. An example of this is scientific and mathematical proofs, which require rigour to the deduction process and follow the WIKID POWER process. Practice with logic and proofs helps to develop rational thinking.

A key point to reflect on is an understanding that the frontal lobe deals primarily with the WIKID POWER transformation processes, and is primarily responsible for converting *data* to *information* to *knowledge* to *intelligence* to *wisdom*.

BECAUSE AND THEREFORE

Many people use their frontal lobe without much thought as to how it works. It's intuitive. It's reasoning. It's rationale. It's logic. Two of the words that often result from the frontal lobe doing its work are "because" and "therefore". Although they seem similar in context, they are fundamentally different in the way they operate.

"Because" is about the past; "therefore" is about the future.

When you use "because", you are concluding matters from the past. For instance:

- The cake burned because it was left it in the oven too long.
- The car engine overheated because the oil wasn't topped up.
- The child slipped on the floor because the shiny floor tiles were wet.
- The woman had difficulty reading because she was too proud to wear glasses.

When you use "therefore", you are concluding matters into the future. For instance,

- The cake recipe indicates a time for the mixture to be in the oven, therefore the cake will burn if left in the oven too long.
- The oil in the engine is low, therefore the engine will overheat and get damaged if it isn't filled up.

- The shiny floor tiles are wet, therefore people may slip if it isn't dried or warning signs installed.
- The magazine and tv have been getting increasingly more difficult to read, therefore glasses are needed.

The use of "because" and "therefore" will help you move up and down through the WIKID POWER transformations. You can use these two words to check your transformations.

ASKING QUESTIONS

The key to stepping through the WIKID POWER transformation process is to keep asking questions and listening to the answers, whether deliberately or intuitively.

A person who can't help but continually ask Why? is naturally attuned and synchronized with the WIKID POWER process. A thirst for *knowledge*, an inquisitive mind, and a desire to excel help make this much easier. Often, such a mind can't help but start solving problems immediately. They yearn for answers and only achieve this by asking questions. For those who are generally more accepting of the world as it is, who don't have an inquisitive mind, this may take practice and the WIKID POWER transformations may only become more obvious when tackling deliberate decision-making exercises.

Regardless of what sort of mind you may have, the key to artfully stepping through the WIKID POWER transformation process is asking yourself some questions, and taking notice of the answers. The WIKID POWER process is about making influential decisions that solve problems. The questions that you ask along the way, and what you do with the answers, help you to determine whether you have enough *knowledge* to deduce *intelligence* and move through to *wise* decisions and *superior power*.

Active Listening

Asking questions is all about obtaining answers to progress the discussion to a successful decision and outcome. Yet how often have you been frustrated by someone who says they hear you, but you feel you haven't been heard? What is the difference between hearing and listening?

The answer to this is in the understanding of active listening, which is a communication technique. It is often used in counselling, negotiating and training because it uses understanding and feedback. Active listening involves:

1. Hearing what the other party says and listening more to the **meaning** and **context** – including identifying any non-verbal signals – than to the words.
2. Feeding back your level of comprehension by **paraphrasing** in your own words what message you think is being communicated to you.
3. Gaining **confirmation** that the message has been correctly understood.
4. **Discussing** the message rather than debating the words.

Of all the times where I have experienced an abrasive interaction, I can usually identify the steps of active listening that have not been taken. In these situations, I often hear one or both of the parties say, "I hear you" or "I understand" but they fail to demonstrate that through paraphrasing, and I often also hear the subsequent response, "no you don't". The saying that something falls on deaf ears suggests of a lack of active listening. When all parties understand and use active listening, these moments disappear, and the matter is usually successfully discussed.

RATEL Procedure

When I first joined the Army, one of the skills that was essential to develop was radio/telephone procedure, known as RATEL procedure.

We learned callsigns, the phonetic alphabet and also how to open and close a conversation over the radio. Of course, it was vital to have radio transmissions as brief as possible to avoid interception, and for the message to be clear, concise and unambiguous. Being in Artillery, it was clear why RATEL procedure was adhered to with zealot-like fervor – one mistake could easily kill many people. Gunners were well-known for their pedantic following and great skills at RATEL.

RATEL procedure is a specific example of active listening. Active listening is a clear example of WIKID POWER and helps to highlight the difference between hearing and listening. Hearing only involves observing *data,* listening takes the transformation up to *knowledge* and *intelligence* and enables further transformations onto the ability to exert influence on the situation (*power*) and reaching a favourable/successful outcome (*superiority*).

Relationships

Aside from unemotional RATEL procedure, there is the everyday emotional interaction of a relationship, whether it be with a child, parent, teacher, boss, client or partner.

When emotions are involved, it is even more vital to practice active listening because that relationship usually contributes to your level of happiness – a great relationship with a boss, client, child or partner certainly makes the world easier. One way to help understand and confirm the message rather than simply hearing the words, is to ask questions that will help you understand the underlying reason, motivation or feeling, for example:
- Can you help me understand what your ideas are?
- Why do you think you were so upset?
- How might we use that idea to move forward?
- What would you think the next step might be?

The Six Interrogatives

Thankfully for us, there is a tried and true set of standard questions which will help get many of the answers to help you onto a decision. These are known as the six interrogatives: What, Why, How, Who, When and Where.

When you start asking these questions, you will find you start pulling together many of the pieces of *knowledge* you need to draw out the *intelligence* that will lead to *wisdom*, *power* and, ideally, *superiority*.

Five Why Technique

The Five Why technique uses an iterative approach to determining cause and effect, and has a primary goal of determining the root cause of a problem. Not surprisingly, it suggests you ask "why?" five times to get the real answers.

I saw it demonstrated with amazing results when Jack Zufelt was presenting on stage and asked volunteers to come up and tell him their core desires. I was shocked that he didn't accept any of their first answers and instead, kept asking why – over and over – until he found out their true desire. At first, I thought it was a tad rude of him, but as he dug deeper, it became quite clear he was getting much closer to their real desires. On two occasions, tears were shed as he uncovered their true core desires.

The Five Why technique helps you cycle the *knowledge* until useful *intelligence* is produced. In the case of WIKID POWER, going through this exercise will help establish the "because" reasons of past actions and the "because" rationale for future options.

Because and Therefore Revisited

As every parent knows, the answer to "Why?" is always "Because . . ." But using "because?" and "therefore?" as questions also helps in planning. The more you ask those questions, the more you see options. As you address more options, you build a more robust plan.

WIKID POWER was devised in G building as I worked to find ways to plan my $30 million annual software budget. I soon found that it had greater application than merely planning. Yet planning uses WIKID POWER whether intentionally or not. If it is used intentionally, planning becomes much more effective, and efficient.

Unfortunately, superficial planning is what I see often. Some people are simply satisfied being able to claim they have planned and in more formal situations, may be able to point to a document collecting dust on a coffee table or bookshelf. However, true planning requires looking at all the options available. Having patience and discipline to do this thoroughly will produce better plans with more chance of success.

It is sometimes difficult for people to realise just how much impact this has, so I encourage you to put the book down for a minute and do this quick exercise to see how much further you get when asking "because?" and "therefore?".

1. Think of what you ate for your last meal.
2. Repetitively ask "because?" until you understand your real reason for the option.
3. Now repeat the exercise but repetitively ask "therefore?" instead.
4. Note:
    a. "Because?" takes you back in time to understand motivation.

b. "Therefore?" takes you forward in time to understand future options.
c. It doesn't take too many repetitions to get better answers.

Asking "because?" and "therefore?" not only helps in everyday life but also in corporate planning. When I was facilitating decision-making meetings using the GDSS, I was often called to facilitate a corporate plan. It became so frequent, I wrote a Corporate Planning Workbook which listed all the theoretical issues to consider on the left facing pages, while the right facing pages had boxes that allowed participants to write their ideas as they related to their situation. It was a great tool and an impressive workbook, if I say so myself! It kept us focussed and therefore produced much better answers because we kept questioning initial responses.

That time was also a time of great improvement efforts, and when Army decided to redesign the Army Corporate Planning System (ACPS) I was a member of the small team asked to make it happen. We considered various methods in designing the new system. One thing that seems mandatory in any decision or planning, especially corporate and military planning, is analysis of the situation. Many people have heard of a SWOT analysis, but I had realised this was not enough.

So What, SWOT, SoWOT and COWS

So What?

As Officers in the Army, we were required to quickly analyse a situation, consider options, make decisions and produce plans quickly. We would go on numerous training exercises, where we would simply go through this planning process over and over. We would present our plans to our syndicate and be grilled on how we came up with the plan. We would also go through various "what if" exercises.

Early in our efforts, weaknesses in our plans were always highlighted with ease. We didn't really know how to come to the incredible deductions (*intelligence*) of our instructors. Over time, we were taught the simplicity of it: keep asking yourself "So What?" For instance:

- The enemy has a howitzer. So What?
- They always travel as a battery of six. So What?
- They are therefore with an infantry Battalion. So What?
- We're outnumbered. So What?
- You can guess where this leads ...

In the case of WIKID POWER, going through the same exercise will help establish the "therefore" answers aimed at the future. These "therefore" answers help to compile a plan.

SWOT

An extension of the "So What?" exercise is a more structured approach that is primarily conducted to determine what the competitive landscape looks like for a business before the options are considered and a plan drawn up. This is commonly known as a SWOT Analysis and is broken down into

- Influences
    - Internal   within the organization's control
    - External   beyond the organization's control
- Impacts
    - Positive   beneficial to the organization
    - Negative   detrimental to the organization

It is best represented in a SWOT matrix as follows.

		Impacts	
		Positive	**Negative**
Influences	**Internal**	Strengths	Weaknesses
	External	Opportunities	Threats

The objective of the WIKID POWER transformation process is to make a decision and plan of action that will influence an environment and ideally gain superiority. Having a sound *knowledge* of the influences and impacts on the organization is critical to solid *intelligence* and great *wisdom*.

The structured approach of a SWOT analysis helps.

APEST and SoWOT
For a completely thorough analysis, each of the SWOT elements needed to apply a further checklist of considerations.
- Adversary
- Political
- Economic
- Social
- Technical

This is known by the acronym APEST and although it is often mentioned, I have rarely seen it implemented to maximum effect. Yet time and time again, I would see a SWOT analysis in a plan that would sit alone and not have any further part to play in the plan. I could not understand why a SWOT analysis was done and included in the plan if it wasn't used. My only conclusion was that consultants thought it needed to be done but didn't understand what to do with it.

So I applied WIKID POWER to the problem, and thought back to what I was taught in Tactical Exercises Without Troops (TEWTs) about asking "So What?". Suddenly, I had two pieces of *knowledge* that made sense and I quickly concluded the *intelligence* that the SWOT analysis needed to produce conclusions that contributed to the plan further. And the way to do this was by asking "So What?" As soon as I implemented this into my planning sessions, the SWOT analysis came to life. The extended analysis led onto other conclusions and the plan addressed all the issues raised in the SWOT analysis. This technique quickly gained a nickname from me and became known as the SoWOT analysis.

Without SoWOT, a SWOT analysis is wasted effort.

COWS

As a group decision facilitator, I enjoyed helping the development of many dozens of plans and as SWOT was continually used, I noticed a flaw in its design.

There were external influences other than threats which negatively impacted the organization. These were constraints. For instance, legal red tape is not an external threat, but is often a negative constraint on a business. Some legislations also imposed negative constraints. So, I changed "threats" to "constraints" which still included threats, since a threat can constrain your actions and chance of success.

At about the same time, I also became aware of a group dynamic regarding morale during the facilitation of plans. People preferred to be uplifted after the exercise rather than down-in-the-mouth. They preferred to deal with the negative impacts first and the positive impacts last. They also preferred to first deal with influences outside their control and end with influences inside their control. This then changed the order I dealt with the analysis to:

		Impacts	
		Negative	**Positive**
Influences	**External**	Constraints	Opportunities
	Internal	Weaknesses	Strengths

I no longer did a SWOT analysis, I did a COWS analysis.

APEST and "So What?" are still applied to the COWS analysis, to ensure a more thorough interrogation of all perspectives and to achieve conclusions that lead to a better production of plans.

As I facilitated many group decision-making meetings, it became clear that having a structured approach worked well because it was logical. The structured framework helped people to see different perspectives and bring forth ideas that were previously untapped. What wasn't quite obvious was why people would suddenly identify many issues and contributions when a new situation or perspective was mentioned, whereas prior to the mention, the ideas weren't forthcoming. In other words, how do you find all the golden information?

FINDING GOLD

How do you find the *data* and *information* that you require to make superior decisions and obtain *superiority*? Sometimes it is there in plain sight but you can't recognise it – often because of your perspective. Sometimes you need to dig to find it – this is the most common method for finding it.

On the military battlefield, patrols are sent out to conduct reconnaissance. On a larger scale, strategic national interests use orbiting satellites to deliver all sorts of photographic and sensory *data* to be analysed and converted into *information, knowledge, intelligence* and, ideally, *wise* decisions to achieve *power* and *superiority*.

While most of us don't have ready access to patrols or satellites, we do have very powerful tools at our disposal that weren't available a few decades ago. The incredible advances in computing power has led to an insatiable demand for *data* to produce *information* and *knowledge* which can be analysed to deduce *intelligence* that can be used to make *wise* decisions.

We can use our computers to scour the Internet for incredible amounts of *data* and *information* that was once only ever dreamed about. The breathtaking advances in computing have also allowed us to analyse the *data* much faster and better than ever to produce stunning *intelligence*.

Moments of Truth

In 2005, the Chairman, President and CEO of Procter & Gamble, A.G. Lafley, coined the terms for the first and second Moments of Truth, and later added a third:

> *"Moments of Truth (MOT) in marketing, is the moment when a customer/user interacts with a brand, product or service to form or change an impression about that particular brand, product or service."*

They are:
- **First moment of truth (FMOT):** When a customer is confronted with the product in-store or in real life.
- **Second moment of truth (SMOT):** When a customer purchases a product and experiences its quality as per the promise of the brand.
- **Third moment of truth (TMOT):** When a consumer gives feedback or reacts towards a brand, product or service i.e. the consumer becomes a brand advocate and gives back via word of mouth or social media publishing.

Yet Google believed people were experiencing a Moment of Truth before these three, and in 2011 added:
- **Zero Moment of truth (ZMOT)** refers to the research which is conducted online about a needed product or service before taking any action i.e. searching for reviews before making a purchase. According to research conducted by Google, 88% of US customers are researching online before actually buying a product, and people checked 10.4 sources of information to make a decision in 2011, almost double the number of sources a year earlier.

Google, the most pervasive of the converters of Internet *data* into valuable *information* and *knowledge,* has come up with some amazing *intelligence* that helps us now identify where to collect that precious *data to aid the decision-making process.* Pure gold!

Reticular Activating System

Sometimes, people dig for valuable *data* and *information* for ages only to suddenly identify many issues and contributions when a particular situation or perspective was mentioned, whereas prior to the mention, these nuggets of gold weren't obvious.

The best way to explain why things may suddenly become apparent is to give you an example.

1. Look around you and observe the things in your environment for about 10 seconds.
   This will enable you to get a head start, being observant and noticing objects nearby. Here's an opportunity to demonstrate your observation skills.
2. Now don't look at your surrounds. Close your eyes.
3. Recall all the orange things.
   To almost everyone, they rattle off maybe two to five. Depending on your environment, this would be usual.
4. Now look up at your surrounds again and see how many there really are.

Again, most people are shocked at how quickly all these objects now jump out at them. It's a filter. It's called the Reticular Activating System (RAS). RAS is the same mechanism that kicks in just after you buy a car and suddenly notice how many there are on the street, whereas before you didn't notice how common they were.

RAS is composed of several neuronal circuits connecting the brainstem to the cortex and is responsible for regulating arousal, sleep-wake transition, mental wakefulness and alertness. A change from a state of deep sleep to wakefulness is helped by RAS. The RAS also helps transitions from relaxed wakefulness to periods of high attention. It is the RAS that is functioning when you are alerted to something.

It is the RAS that is invoked when you write something important down to remember it, or you use imagery to peg an idea to a memory, or you use affirmations to help you achieve your goals. Many years before RAS was first investigated, Napoleon Hill wrote:

> *"The moment you write out a statement of your chief aim, you have planted an image of that firmly in your subconscious mind. Through some process that even the most enlightened scientists have not yet discovered, Nature causes your subconscious mind use that chief aim as a pattern or blueprint guiding the major portion of your thoughts, ideas and efforts towards the attainment of your objective."*

By using WIKID POWER deliberately, more things will become apparent thanks to the RAS. As you keep asking questions and looking at different perspectives, you will enjoy many revelations.

This was my very experience as I looked into the various stages of the *information* transformation process. All of a sudden, theories leapt out at me and examples sprung to life. The result is a clear and thorough WIKID POWER process that addresses large cross-sections of life experiences, especially decision-making.

THE THREE EFFS

Whilst developing aspects of Army's strategic plan for information management a small group of key people were sitting around a rickety table, brainstorming some issues. At one stage, I asked what the purpose of Army's IT was and the answer "better decisions" was not enough for me. I probed further and asked "What type of decisions?" Two thirds of the answer I was expecting: effective and efficient.

The decisions needed to be effective in that they achieved what was required. In other words, "did it do the job?" If the answer returned was "yes", then it was effective.

Yet being effective was not enough. It might make some people happy if the job was done, but others certainly wanted to know if the resources invested in the solution were used in the best possible manner. In business terms, this is known as Return On Investment (ROI). To others, it is simply efficiency.

I was surprised to hear a colleague speak up after the chatter died down. He said that it also needed to have efficacy. In other words, it needed to be presented acceptably. Solutions need to be acceptable to others by having efficacy. I have seen many effective and efficient solutions fail because they were too complicated, ahead of their time or the end users didn't like them! In other words, they did not have efficacy.

Hence, check the *wisdom* resulting from your WIKID POWER transformation has, what I call, the three Effs: Effective, Efficient, Efficacious.

CONVERTING FROM HUMAN TO ELECTRONIC – AND BACK

One of the archaic traditions that existed when I arrived at Army Headquarters was the tea lady. At mid-morning, she would work her way around G building with a trolley and trays of goodies to buy for morning tea. She would stop near my office which was in the centre of the Eastern side of G building and everyone from that side would gather around for their supplies. The next three stories are from my morning tea gang.

Destruction of Knowledge

One of the most startling things that happened to me within weeks of starting at Army Headquarters was when I met a senior officer who was retiring. He had been responsible for hardware, as I was for software. I walked into his office for a chat as he was packing up his belongings. He had been there quite a while and his office had become quite a comfortable and personalized haven in a stark grey environment. He was emptying his bookshelf, and had cleared his computer's hard drive as required. I asked him where I could find his work when he was gone, and he said that it was all in his head. There were no *physical* or *electronic* records. He was the *human* expert that people consulted – and he was leaving.

Loss of Knowledge

On the same side of G building, on the same floor, about ten offices away, I visited the Army Scientific Liaison Officer (SLO is not a designation I would've wanted), who was the principal adviser regarding science. I admired his *knowledge* – he was obviously very well read, as evidenced by a huge stack of document boxes piled high in the corners of his office. He had amazing *information* from the Defence Science and Technology Organisation (DSTO). I had an issue I thought he could help with and asked him if he had any ideas. He went to a pile, opened a box and pulled out a file for me. Stunned that he knew where everything was amongst the apparent ramble that I saw, I asked whether there was a catalogue of it all. "No"! Naively, I asked how I would find anything if he was hit by a bus, and he looked at me despairingly.

Access to Knowledge

Another colleague believed it was his role to be the sole repository of *knowledge* on his specialty. I challenged him about the coding system he used that precluded anyone else from accessing his *information*. Unlike the previous two examples, who were oblivious to the consequences of lost *knowledge* when they left, this colleague was deliberately denying access to others.

These three examples above drove me to work to ensure Army collected *information* electronically so that it was always accessible to others. The importance of converting physical and human *knowledge* into an electronic form was driven home. My work to build a well-structured *information* source was critical for decision-making.

Value of Knowledge

As I write these stories, I can't help but include another, similar story from shortly after I left the Army. My work in Army had become known and I was headhunted to model the processes for the Olympics using the Group Decision Support System (GDSS) for Business Process Modelling (BPM). I had developed a long list of modifications that made the exercise much more rewarding with many different uses and formats for the output.

One of the uses of my BPM modifications was the production of a requirements analysis for software systems and I was asked to produce the requirements for the system that would be used by the large media contingents. This required collaboration between two of the most powerful stakeholders in Olympic planning: the techies and the media. One Olympics after another, they would be at each other's throats, claiming that the other party didn't understand their perspective. Neither were happy with the existing solutions, and neither believed they could resolve the issues.

I approached the gurus, and asked if they could participate in a group *knowledge* collating exercise, aimed at producing user requirements for the Olympic media software application. They were aghast. If they freely offered their valuable *knowledge,* to be collected and reused without them, they would be redundant. They would be out of work and off the gravy train that the Olympics offered. Their exclusive, invaluable and irreplaceable *knowledge* provided them with a *powerful* and influential leverage to ensure their continued involvement – under lucrative conditions. It ensured their success and *superiority*.

One way or another, I managed to help them see that their attendance was an acknowledgement of their authority. They all showed up wearing with pride like campaign ribbons, their security card lanyards from the various games they had attended – Nagano,

Atlanta, Lillehammer, Barcelona, Albertville, Seoul, Calgary, Los Angeles.

The session went marvelously well, and before long, the previously combatting parties were sharing jokes as they ploughed through the work. I produced the requirements document the next day and it was sent to the coders in Spain for converting into the application.

Three memorable bits of feedback were received:
1. The coders told me it was the best requirements document they had seen.
2. The workshop participants told me it went so well, they didn't really need me. A nice but backhanded compliment which is the frustration of good facilitators.
3. The gurus had their expertise recognized and were in greater demand, giving them a sense of greater importance.

By converting human *knowledge* into *data* and *information* electronically and then physically, we enabled a much wider audience to access and use *information* – to transform it further through WIKID POWER and into *power* and *superiority*.

The value of human *knowledge* is leveraged when converted into physical and electronic forms for greater access.

TIMING

The timing of decisions is vital in many situations. Success happens with both serendipity and planning.

Two sayings collide for me about timing: "It's funny that the harder I work, the luckier I get." and "Luck is where opportunity meets preparation."

The key to making timely, quick decisions is preparation.

OODA Loop

The timely gathering of *information* helps to ensure that *information* can be quickly accessed and easily used by anyone anywhere in order to make quick decisions.

> "An adequate decision on time
> is better than a perfect decision too late."

This saying highlights the importance of timely decisions in maintaining *superiority*. *Superiority* relies on influencing the situation through superior *power* thereby controlling an adversary's reactions. This requires timely access to *information* to ensure *information* is transformed to *power* quicker than the time it takes for an adversary to transform *information* into *power* for themselves. This is known as reducing the time of the decision cycle.

The decision cycle is also known as the OODA Loop (the acronym for Observe, Orientate, Decide, Act) or the Boyd Cycle after the man that proposed it. The OODA Loop describes where decisions fit into a controlling process, whether innate or learned, immediate or deliberate, reflexive or intuitive.

The OODA Loop begins when an event is observed in an environment, the ramifications of the event comprehended through orientation, a decision made and an action taken. To have *superiority* over an adversary, your decision cycle must be quicker than your adversary's. This ensures the adversary reacts to your decisions and actions, and that you have taken another action before your adversary has observed and countered the situation you have influenced. By maintaining a controlling influence, *power* and *superiority* are achieved. WIKID POWER builds on and extends the OODA Loop concept.

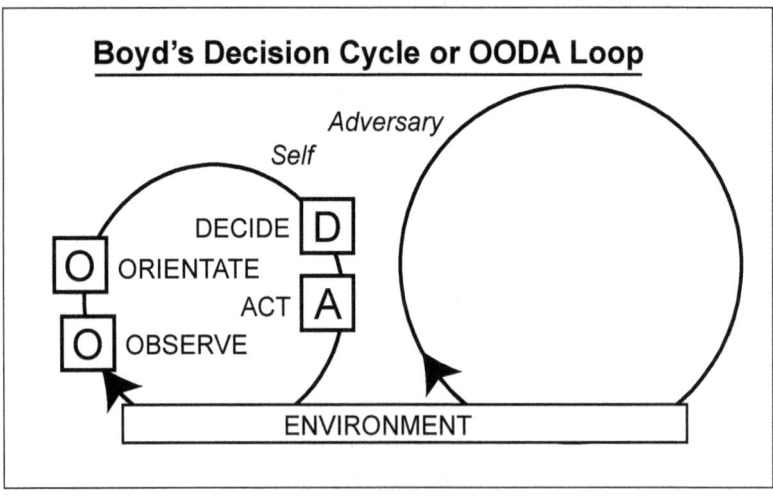

Lucky Information Hastens a Superior Decision
I had been posted to the Ready Reaction Force and was in a hotel room, awaiting the removals truck to arrive with my belongings. On the morning of the day the truck was arriving, as I was preparing to leave the hotel, I heard the phone ring. There was an urgent call-up and I had to return to base immediately.

We were informed there was an incident at a mine on a Pacific Island and we had to protect and evacuate our national citizens who were being directly threatened by armed and dangerous locals. We were issued all our ammunition and were fully "bombed-up" and sitting on our packs awaiting transport. The aircraft was on the runway with engines turning. As we were in the briefing room for final orders, a fellow Officer said, "What mine is that?" After the reply, his jaw dropped and his eyes popped like organ-stops. His sister was married to the mine manager.

He indicated that he could call her to get a more accurate, reliable and up-to-date picture of the situation. That phone call revealed that the incident was wildly exaggerated and that there was no concern for their safety whatsoever – they were not impacted. A large number of troops stood down and a serious incident was serendipitously avoided.

Managing *information* for accuracy, and in a timely manner, can be a serious matter.

The Three Fs

There are three Fs (as opposed to the three Effs homophone mentioned earlier) that relate directly to the OODA Loop: Fight, Flight or Freeze. First described in 1932 and now often called the fight or flight response, it is a physiological reaction to a perceived harmful event, attack or threat to survival.

The response is determined by the perceived control over the situation or environment. Control of the environment can be determined by WIKID POWER / OODA Loop, and how quickly you can cycle through the transformations to be proactively participating in the environment with *power* at a faster rate than the threat. If you can, then you are controlling any adversary that is slower at processing and hence reactive to your observed actions.

The fight, flight or freeze response is simply your perceived ability to cycle through the WIKID POWER transformation more frequently and faster than the threat, and ultimately to control the situation and gain *superiority*.

In essence, should you believe your abilities can overcome the situation, you are likely to fight. If you believe they are not enough to prevent harm, you might flee. If you believe it will result in unknown consequences, or you believe you can neither fight nor flee, you might freeze. The freeze response can also be when the *information* processing is too overwhelming.

However, the three Fs are primarily unproductive responses and unhelpful when we are looking for a productive way forward. In some situations, instead of fighting, fleeing or freezing, which all indicate unproductive approaches, we could instead choose to face and fix the issues in a positive and productive approach to the situation. This would require a few more deliberate iterations of WIKID POWER to overcome the intuitive decision to fight, flee or freeze. Extra iterations might include wondering about any *knowledge* of what might remove a roadblock, the intentions of the solution, what the priorities are and the goal. We can now refer to the three Fs as the five Fs which comprise both productive and unproductive responses as well as reflexive and deliberate responses: fight, flight, freeze, face, fix. They are all decisions, but with quite different expectations of the outcome.

Anxiety and Decision-Making

Anxiety and the three Fs go hand-in-hand since the three Fs are reactions to anxiety or stress. Recent research by neuroscientists at the University of Pittsburgh has identified the neural networks that disrupt decision-making during anxiety. The research focussed on various parts of the brain.

The prefrontal cortex (PFC) which is in the frontal lobes of the cerebrum is the most recent to evolve and has a key role in executive functions such as long-term planning, understanding rules, calculating the consequences of risk and reward, regulating emotions, problem-solving and decision-making. Neurons in the PFC are disrupted by anxiety. One conclusion of the research was that anxiety often leads to poor decision-making.

The researchers also found that the orbitofrontal cortex (OFC) brain region, which plays a role in problem solving and learns through trial and error, did not appear impacted by anxiety. They discovered the relationship of the OFC to problem-solving by photographing brain images of mice in real-time as they learned how-to problem solve through trial and error. The OFC was dramatically resculpted during the problem-solving process of active learning.

Other studies of anxiety and decision-making have focussed on Cortisol production which is enhanced in times of stress or anxiety. The studies concluded that many leaders have low levels of Cortisol during stress indicating an ability to stay calm under pressure, while others may exhibit high levels of Cortisol during stress indicating an inability to stay calm. Cortisol levels, partly due to stress or anxiety, help explain the three Fs and why some people appear to stay calm and make better decisions under stressful circumstances.

Get A Round Tuit

Sadly, it often takes far too long before people realize that they need to take action to help ensure *superiority*. A common example that many can relate to is when a computer crashes and they lose valuable information. Their backup wasn't done as recently as hoped, or at all. I can no longer recall where I heard it, but in almost all cases, people wish they had earlier got "a round tuit". It is more commonly known as procrastination.

Procrastination stops the progress of the WIKID POWER transformation process. It steps in and prevents *wisdom* being converted into *power*. It is the avoidance of action and participation. When procrastination exists, *superiority* won't.

One of Napoleon Hill's tenets was that successful people make decisions quickly and change their minds slowly, while unsuccessful people make decisions slowly and change their minds quickly. Quick decisions and actions prevent procrastination from stealing success. Napoleon Hill, Jack Zufelt and Matthew Micalewicz all claim desire as a driving motivation to taking action. When I look back on the things in my life where I procrastinated, it is clear to see that my desire to take action is not strong. When I look at the things in my life where I have taken quick decisive action that leads to success, it is equally clear that I have had a passionate desire about those matters and my preparation was simply looking for an opportunity to take action. When that opportunity presented itself, which is easy to see through the Reticular Activating System, it was quite simple to take quick, decisive action because of the alignment with my objectives that follow my desires. There's a common saying: "Procrastination is the thief of time." Yet it should also be noted that:

"Procrastination is the thief of *power* and *superiority.*"

What Happened?

Closely related to procrastination is apathy. If you don't care about something, there is clearly no passion or desire.

>Success finds those who seek it.

Apathy and procrastination prevent people from seeking success. If success isn't sought out, it is unlikely to jump out in front of you and land on your doorstep.

There is a saying:

> "There are those that make things happen,
> there are those that watch things happen and
> there are those that wonder what on earth just happened."

The apathetic and procrastinators don't make things happen. Only those who take decisions to actively participate in their particular environment find *power*. And when you have *power* that succeeds in achieving your goals, you have *superiority*, or control. When you leave control to others, or watch things happening rather than taking control, it is like being a cork on an ocean bobbing around at the mercy of the elements. In the end, you'll end up wondering what happened. Often, the outcomes aren't what you'd wish for.

Psychologists will tell you that when people take control, they are generally less anxious, more relaxed and much happier. Yet, paradoxically, it is often too difficult and overwhelming to attempt to take control of everything. Some things need to go through to the keeper. It is often more relaxing and effective if you pick your battles. There is a military saying that is commonly found in business, negotiation and relationship advice:

> "You don't have to win every battle to win the war."

PRIORITIES

Priorities help determine which battles to pick and focus on. Priority setting is an important aspect of working out what opportunities to choose with *wisdom* during the WIKID POWER transformation process. Priorities help you plan to take control.

Importance

When I was in G building and considering all the issues I wanted to deal with, a colleague showed me a great way to determine my priorities.

He showed me a simple 2 x 2 table like the one below:

Urgent	High	C	A
	Medium	D	B
		Medium	High
		Important	

When I asked the inevitable question "What about Low?" he looked at me with a smug grin and said "Ian, why would you ever consider prioritizing something that was Low?"

He said that all you do is tackle the issues from A to D. I was confused and asked why I should tackle something with high importance and low urgency (B) before I tackled something with greater urgency (C). He kept his smug look, but with a kind tone, pointed out that if I kept focusing on the important issues, the urgent ones will disappear! How true he was.

In hindsight, I can now correlate "importance" with "desires". The higher a desire, the higher the importance. Setting priorities is easier when importance and desire are considered.

With regards to detail and granularity, there are three types of plans where priorities need to be considered carefully:
- Long Term   Strategic   focused on big concepts
- Medium Term   Operational   from concepts to projects
- Short Term   Tactical   detail / conduct of tasks within a project

When discussing financial plans, a similar concept is seen.
- Long term based on about three years
- Medium term based on annual matters
- Short term based on day-to-day management and monthly targets

Without the longer-term plans, the medium and short term plans are directionless and goals are unlikely to be achieved.

Work needs to be consistently and concurrently conducted on all three plans simultaneously and without pause on any of them if control is to be expected.

After going to an inspirational weekend where a whole new set of desired plans rushed at her, a young colleague asked me how I balance them all. What I told her has worked for me is to firstly have them written down and to understand your core desires. Then to commit to having worked on at least one long, medium and short term issue every week. It is amazing how quickly a to do list can be completed when a little bit of focus and progress is made every week.

Risk

When facilitating planning sessions, I added another method for deciding on priorities. Risk Analysis.

There is risk in everything. Risk cannot be eliminated, but can be managed. I found that despite entrepreneurial flare, risk management is always an issue that is considered for business viability. The word for ignoring risk is gambling. Whether starting up an enterprise or keeping something going, risk should be regularly assessed, and plans adjusted accordingly.

When assessing risk, there are two key elements that provide the springboard for further analysis: Likelihood and Consequences

Likelihood is the assessed chance of something happening, often expressed as a percentage but also expressed more simply such as high and low. Consequences are an assessment of the impact should the situation happen. They are always expressed consistently for all issues being assessed. For instance, it may be the financial impact, loss of jobs, fatalities or anything else. They may be expressed simply such as low to high, or with more granularity using a different scale.

Likelihood and consequences are usually drawn on two axes of a graph or table. A simple way to assess risk is to multiply the numerical value of each axis – the higher the number, the higher the risk.

				Impact			
Likelihood	Very High	5	5	10	15	20	25
	High	4	4	8	12	16	20
	Medium	3	3	6	9	12	15
	Low	2	2	4	6	8	10
	Very Low	1	1	2	3	4	5
	value		1	2	3	4	5
			Very Low	Low	Medium	High	Very High

Naturally, you address the highest risk matters, the ones with the largest number, first by asking the common question:

> "What's the worse that can happen?"

To manage risk, there is another saying that helps keep the detail focused.

> "Plan for the worst, hope for the best!"

If risk has been planned well, the rewards will reflect that.

Consideration of risks are the *intelligence* component of WIKID POWER, and the rewards are ideally *superiority*.

Reward

In economics, there is a principle known as the Law of Diminishing Returns. The idea is that you keep taking reducing profits until there is no more profit to take. Most people know this concept as picking the low hanging fruit, where you take the easy wins first and keep going, but the further you go, the harder you work for the same reward.

The same concept is used as for risk, when calculating expected rewards. In the discipline of operational research, this is the basis of decision trees and expected reward. Simply by multiplying the probability of something happening by the reward should it happen. For instance, should the conversion rate of potential customers be 10%, and 200 customers walk in the door, you would expect 20 sales.

For the best implementation of WIKID POWER, priorities need to be considered carefully when considering the *intelligence* and working out which opportunities to decide upon, most likely the ones with the best reward. Considering priorities will help produce better *wisdom*.

Results

I spent a day with my sister in her business advisory enterprise. She was going away for a holiday and asked if I could step in for her as CEO for a short while. During our handover, she gave a presentation to business owners where she asked them to draw a circle with spokes like a bicycle wheel. She then labeled each spoke for each area of business and asked them to assess how they performed on each one – with 0/10 being at the hub and 10/10 being on the rim. After the exercise, she enlightened them that for a smoother ride, they needed to have a smoother wheel without radical bumps – this represented balance. She also enlightened them that naturally, they would go faster and be more efficient in their ride if their wheel was bigger, representing the idea to get better results in all areas by aiming for 10/10.

Many months later, I was enlightened about an idea to represent not only results, but importance on the same bicycle wheel. As I was advising business owners and CEOs at the time, I tried this out and almost without exception, the graphs of the results and importance wheels looked nothing like each other. In other words, people were often obtaining great results in areas of lesser importance and vice-versa, people were getting poor results in areas of great importance.

SHIFT ME NOW

One of my best school friends was rapidly climbing the global business ladder and had become the first non-American VP of one of the world's largest corporations. We didn't see as much of each other as we used to, but on one occasion I recall, while discussing one of the books he authored on fatherhood, he mentioned how interesting it is that people spend little time on the things that are of greatest importance. This revelation caused me to add yet another jagged circle to my bicycle wheel – effort.

The incongruences between the three circles indicate where priorities may need to be addressed. Anywhere a spoke has three different values, for importance, effort and results, you should consider more carefully what is happening there. Go through the WIKID POWER process, by observing more *data*, collecting the *information*, assessing additional bits of *knowledge* to produce better *intelligence* about what is happening. Make *wiser* decisions about how to address it so that you can influence a situation by taking action to exercise your *power and gain control*. Ideally, you will become successful in areas of various importance and achieve appropriate results by applying the appropriate effort. That's WIKID POWER!

The example of the SHIFT ME NOW$_{TM}$ graph is shown here. For ease of memory, I have used the spokes of the wheel, common areas of personal desire, in my acrostic to remind you of your overriding desire. Notice in the example shown in the diagram how some spokes appear relatively consistent with their results, importance and effort, whilst others indicate an inconsistent or incongruent approach? It is clear to see where some effort is too much, and some is too little. The SHIFT ME NOW$_{TM}$ analysis helps you allocate priorities to achieve personal success.

The same concept may be applied to any environment or situation. For instance, business may have different spokes representing goals or functional areas and military may have different spokes representing various elements of an operation.

SHIFT ME NOW™

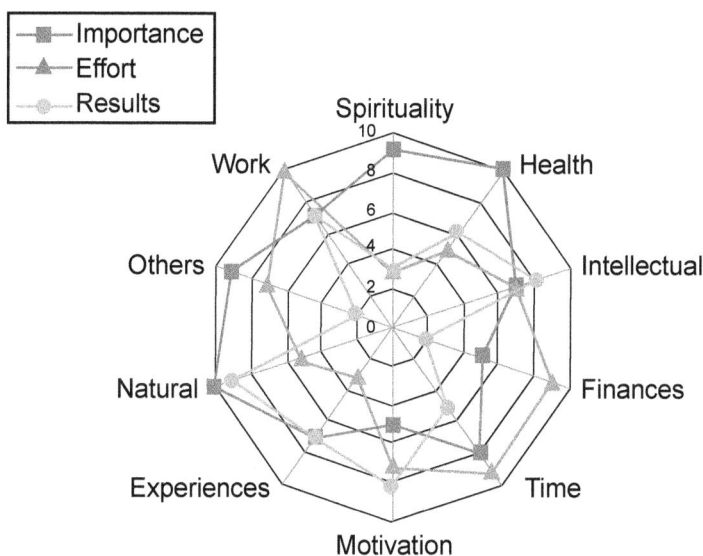

Tips for Using WIKID POWER in Practice   139

BEHAVIOR

How people respond and behave is critical in assisting the decision-making process. How you respond to those people is also vital. Understanding various behaviors and responses is the focus of the next section.

Behaviors, Attitudes, Values, Beliefs

Behaviors are indications of attitudes and values. Values are indicators of beliefs. People behave according to their attitude which is driven by their values and beliefs.

Personal insight and self-awareness is needed for behaviors to be the result of *superior* decision-making processes. Awareness of personal cognitive biases certainly helps identify where emotional or irrational weightings are assigned to *knowledge* being assessed to produce *intelligence*.

Beliefs are ideas that are considered true, based on certain evidence (from themselves or others such as religion and society) or probabilities, and are something people are willing to defend. An example is the belief that there is life after death.

Values reflect important beliefs. They are standards by which to guide a commitment to attitude and behavior. Values need to be well understood to make clear, rational, responsible and consistent decisions. An example of a value is that because a person believes there is life after death, they need to be nice to others, which will ensure a better life after death than would result from being nasty.

Where there is ambivalence or uncertainty about values, poor decisions and behavior is more likely to follow. For individuals and organizations, it is vital to understand and believe in values that guide decisions and attitudes.

Attitudes are the mental disposition shown towards a situation and others prior to making a decision. Attitudes are closely related to cognitive bias and can result in poorly considered decisions. Some factors, unrecognized as beliefs and values, can influence attitudes in decision-making such as personality traits or biases. An example of an attitude is a desire to never criticize, even constructively, since it is not nice.

With any decision, whether an individual or group decision, it is important to consider the beliefs, values, attitudes and behaviors of all stakeholders. Without such consideration, a decision is unlikely to have buy-in, and will most likely not succeed.

Honestly . . . is honesty a value?
When facilitating the many dozens of strategic plans during my group decision support system time, values always loomed as an early issue to decide.

In one particular session, someone suggested honesty to be a value that needed to be articulated. My great mentor and friend chipped in with his ever-so-dry wit and said, "Would you consider a stated value of being dishonest?"

His point was clear that it is more impacting if values are ones that differentiate you from others and indicate a preference from other possible options. Dishonesty was not a possible option for many, so it did not differentiate and hence ruled honesty out as a value to specify!

Social Information Processing

Social information processing relates to how people establish social relationships. Studies show which parts of the brain are engaged during various stages of social interaction and what actions take place in what order.

Initial research in 1996 by Crick and Dodge primarily focused on children, showing that children relate facial expressions of anonymous people with past experiences. Other observations are also included such as body language and voice control in determining how to behave in a social situation.

Emotion and cognition are the two forms of social information processing. Emotional processing is based on motivation and cognitive processing is based on *knowledge*.

The social information processing model identifies various social behaviors people process in sequence which include deciphering and understanding social signs, outlining goals, creations of response, decision of action, and behavior of action. It shows that people perform a series of mental operations in a social situation:

1. they perceive the various features of the situation and comprehend the relevant ideas,
2. they try to attribute the information to every participant,
3. they generate answers, and
4. they select a response to finally act out the behavior.

I'll leave it to you to draw the similarities with WIKID POWER.

Napoleon Hill's Laws of Success

Napoleon Hill was perhaps the founder of motivational material from the 1920s, and wrote the seminal book on success, a project initiated by his editor Andrew Carnegie, one of the most successful people of the era.

I have taken the following quotes out of his book *The Magic Ladder to Success*:

- "gather, classify and organize the useful knowledge that is essential for success"
- "power is simply organized knowledge, expressed through intelligent action!"
- "Knowledge, general in nature and unorganized, is not power; it is only potential power – the material out of which real power may be developed."
- "Power grows out of organized knowledge, but, mind you, it grows out of it, through application and use! Someone may become a walking encyclopedia of knowledge without possessing any power. This knowledge becomes power only to the extent that it is organized, classified and put into action"
- "Ford could have waged a battle in industry or finance that would have exterminated those same men, with all their abstract knowledge and wisdom." . . . "Someone who can intelligently use the knowledge . . ."

It is quite clear that Hill grasped the concept of WIKID POWER and would be a strong advocate of the transformation process he incidentally described several times.

Observe, collect and organize data

Data	+	**R**ecognition	=	Information
Information	+	**E**xperience	=	Knowledge
Knowledge	+	**W**onder	=	Intelligence
Intelligence	+	**O**pportunity	=	Wisdom
Wisdom	+	**P**articipation	=	Power

Power is enacted in an environment to gain superiority

Superiority delivers success and victory

Ackoff's Tenses

Russell L Ackoff was a management and organizational theorist in the 70s. He was a pioneer of operations research and systems dynamics and was renowned for combining theory and practice. He proposed the idea that individual systems are driven by a purpose.

Ackoff helped management to realize that although model-building and quantitative analysis is important, it comes after the process of thinking, doesn't replace it and helps to highlight where sloppy thinking occurred. He concluded that an organization's present state is largely determined by what it did in the past, rather than what was done to it, and therefore the future is largely determined by what it does now. He developed a whole synopsis of the various states and tenses.

Ackoff's past, present and future synopsis can be signposted on the WIKID POWER model.

Past	=	Data
	=	Information
	=	Knowledge
Present	=	Intelligence
Future	=	Wisdom
	=	Power
	=	Superiority

In thinking through a problem-solving exercise, remember that "because" is past tense and "therefore" is future tense. Which one(s) apply to the present tense? Problem-solving, planning and WIKID POWER are inextricably linked.

Peter Principle

Collaboratively, Ackoff developed the term "f-Law" in 2006 to describe a series of over 100 distilled observations of poor leadership and the misplaced *wisdom* that often surrounds management in organizations. Interestingly this subversive publication compares well with *The Peter Principle: Why Things Always Go Wrong*, which was co-authored by Lawrence Peter in 1969 and explains why employees only stop being promoted once they can no longer perform effectively – in essence, that "managers rise to the level of their incompetence." In other words, they are promoted because of their skills at one level, but they don't have the management skills for the higher level, and are promoted no further.

The WIKID POWER model explains the Peter Principle as an inability to progress the transformations beyond knowledge.

	=	Data
	=	Information
Promotion basis	=	Knowledge
Inability	=	Intelligence
Incompetence	=	Wisdom
Impotent to act	=	Power
Failure	=	Superiority

When I was in Army Headquarters, I was required to work closely with a senior Officer who was a stonewall to achieving any reform or progress. One day, when I prodded him to make a decision, he quite proudly replied "I didn't get to where I am by making bad decisions." I couldn't help my immediate thought in response "That's because you don't make *any* decisions." He never made any lasting impact and was not promoted any further.

Little Pond to Big Pond

The Peter Principle also partially explains why some people may never leave their childhood neighbourhood – a fear of moving into unknown territory.

When I first joined the Army, I went to the Royal Military College, Duntroon, where there were four classes, one for each year of seniority and each with special privileges. These classes were unofficially known as: dogs of dogs, kings of dogs, dogs of kings, kings of kings. The concept was an indication of status and authority.

It's a common story of a little fish or big fish in a little pond or big pond. Just as you master confidence in your environment, you move onto a new and challenging environment to master.

It mirrors the various situations in life such as transition from primary school to secondary school to college to university, sporting prowess moving from club to area to state to national teams, or progress at work from apprentice to technician to manager to consultant to industry expert.

Some people make the transitions and use the WIKID POWER transformation process to gain *superiority* and control over each situation, while others don't make the next steps through ability, circumstances or fear. Often, it's an attitude.

Attitude often stops people from seeking *knowledge* and skills required to progress to the next environment with success.

Attitude, Skills and Knowledge

When I was contemplating retiring from the Army, I was chatting to a colleague who had transitioned out of Army and into a new career in recruiting. He highlighted to me the acronym ASK, which is what potential employers seek in successful candidates for positions – attitude, skills and knowledge.

After I started my own company, business boomed and it doubled every six months for 30 months. Since I relied heavily on technology for my advantages, I quickly needed a support IT person. I advertised. Many applied for the role and along with my Business Development Manager, we interviewed several. Most had impressive CVs and qualifications, yet I was miffed by one who appeared focused on pay and conditions, hours and holidays. Although the most experienced and qualified, he didn't get the job because of his attitude. After further discussion, we hired someone who was from the hospitality industry, had little IT experience or education but we felt had the right attitude. One afternoon, I asked him to update all the office computers with some difficult new software and he told me that he didn't know how. I went home, devastated that I had hired the wrong person. Next morning, as I arrived to work, early as usual, I saw him working on an office computer. He had gone home, worked through all the issues, found a solution and was implementing it on the last computer as I arrived. He was always an asset that could solve anything I put to him. His attitude overcame his skills and knowledge. We made the right choice.

In the book *Life in Half a Second*, Michalewicz discusses self-belief, which he says is a critical attitude for success. He points to experience and knowledge that help self-belief and a can-do attitude. He equates experience to knowledge and says that, of the five doors that need to be passed through for success, knowledge is the fourth door. He says:

- "... first-time entrepreneurs ... need to acquire the knowledge – either through direct education, hiring experienced people, or both. Without knowledge, failure is the likely result."
- "Lack of knowledge and experience is the primary reason why the majority of new businesses fail within a few years of starting up. First-time entrepreneurs don't know what they don't know."
- "... knowledge and belief ... come from the same place: your environment."
- "Knowledge will empower you."

Michalewicz explains that knowledge is readily available if you have the right attitude to discover it. Success requires the development of a hierarchy of goals and mini-goals; the top goal requiring several mini-goals to achieve. Each mini-goal requiring their own mini-goals. And so on. Start at the bottom-most mini-goals and work your way up. Once you reach the top, start over. The top of that goal pyramid becomes the bottom of the next. Go from little pond to big pond. An attitude of success means you always have new goals to achieve.

When mapped to the WIKID POWER framework, ASK is positioned as follows:

	=	Data
	=	Information
Knowledge	=	Knowledge
Skills	=	Intelligence
Attitude	=	Wisdom
	=	Power
	=	Superiority

Education, Training and Experience

I have kept the acronym ASK close to me ever since I learned it. My position is that you can get knowledge and skills but attitude is different – it's your personality that can change as you experience life.

- Knowledge is gained through education,
- Skills are gained through training, and
- Attitude is gained through experience.

In the teaching industry, there is often a clear distinction between education and training and I like to be clear about that differentiation. To highlight the difference, a degree at university is about educators teaching knowledge, whilst a trade qualification comes through being trained in skills (often on the job and via apprenticeships).

Another example that helps you remember is to imagine you are about to have delicate brain surgery. You ask your surgeon, "How good are you?" A surgeon that has the knowledge and education might answer, "I've read lots of textbooks about it but you're my first patient – don't worry!" Whilst another trained and skilled surgeon might answer, "I've performed hundreds of these, first under the guidance of the best surgeon in the land, and then with my own team. All the operations I've done have been successful." Which one has knowledge and education, and which one is trained and skilled? Which one do you prefer?

Additionally, how would you feel if the last surgeon said, "I'm so good I think I'll take some short cuts this time so that I can get away to my golf game early!" That's attitude.

I have already explained the connection between learning, the frontal lobe, attitude and failure. How everything fits together is becoming quite clear. The "education, training and experience" paradigm are pegged to the WIKID POWER model as follows:

			=	Data		
			=	Information		
Education	=	Knowledge	=	Knowledge	=	past
Training	=	Skills	=	Intelligence	=	present
Experience	=	Attitude	=	Wisdom	=	future
			=	Power		
			=	Superiority		

One might also suggest that education teaches about knowledge that's been realized in the past, training is about developing skills in the present, and experience and attitude prepare for the future.

THE GETTING OF WISDOM

I'm reminded of the cartoon about decision-making that depicts a chalkboard with incredibly complex and convoluted diagrams and many arrows, the last arrow pointing to a box that says, "and then a miracle occurs" – meaning nobody really understood how to solve the problem.

The WIKID POWER process holds true for all decisions, but some people want more guidance on the *wisdom* part of it, which they liken to the "and then a miracle occurs" situation.

For some of the most basic decisions, instinct or reflexes work adequately, but for the more complex decisions it would be folly to rely on gut instincts because of the influence of cognitive biases. That section concluded that external perspective, such as subject matter experts, would be advisable. For the most complex of decisions, other perspectives are required to produce *wise* decisions. In the middle, you might simply rely on your own judgement calls instead of instinct or others.

From the least to most complex decisions, the *wisdom* is most likely to come from:
- instincts,
- your own judgement calls and/or
- perspectives from others.

Regardless, the WIKID POWER process still applies and describes how the decisions are made, regardless whether instinct, judgement or perspectives are used heavily.

From a Sneeze to World Domination

SNEEZING

When I first presented WIKID POWER as my intended PhD thesis at university, I had an audience that looked quite casual. Beneath the mask was an assassin armed with deadly questions. All went well until question time.

The first was more of a statement than a question. A smug demeanour spread across the countenance of my first would-be assassin. "*Power* is an evil thing." Having learned as an Officer in the Army to respond to questions with confidence, especially to those you are stumped by, I endeavoured to display a knowing smile while I kicked in another piece of training: breathe, re-state the question, start with what you *know* – and hope an answer will come to mind.

My stance took on a forward, confident position whilst attempting not to look aggressive. "Some do see *power* as an evil thing. Especially where evil is the objective of *power*." I now struggled to work out how to say it without the words "however" or "but" – I didn't want to negate my pitch. "*Power* is the exercise of influence. As the WIKID POWER transformations progress, decisions are made along the way. To participate in an environment is to exercise influence – be it small or large. The aim is to influence so that you succeed. In other words, control the situation or environment. Indeed, this transformation process explains **every** decision and action you take."

And then, as if some anchor on a morning show stepped in with a cleverly crafted segue between stories, another question was fired by another would-be assassin.

"Well then, how does it explain me having a sneeze?"

My mind wanted to express what a cunning question that was, but my transformation model was on the line. I maintained a soft look, at the same time engaging with the others in the audience who were now smiling at the mini-duel that was being staged.

"This is how it works. Your nose starts twitching and those signals are **observed** by your brain as *data*. Your brain **recognizes** those signals as twitches – *information* that puts the signals into context. Because your brain is processing this as your personal **experience**, it is also automatically your *knowledge*. Your brain now **wonders** what this means and attempts to make sense of it by accessing other bits of related *knowledge* it has such as 'When I twitch like this it means I'm going to sneeze.' and 'When I sneeze I spray everywhere unless I use a tissue.' Within a nanosecond, the brain concludes the *intelligence* that you are about to sneeze and you should get a tissue. Applying that **opportunity** to save yourself from mortifying embarrassment, your brain displays great *wisdom* in deciding to get a tissue.

"Here, a few other micro WIKID POWER cycles take place with the resulting action that you **participate** in the situation and exercise *power* to influence the outcome by quickly grabbing a tissue. When you sneeze, you either **succeed** or not from embarrassing yourself with an uncaptured spray. Assuming you've succeeded and achieved your goal, you have shown *superiority* and control over the situation."

I have not been thrown a scenario I couldn't explain easily with the WIKID POWER transformation process. The above example would have taken place in a nanosecond and the WIKID POWER transformation process would have been **instinctive** or **intuitive** and almost unintentional. In more structured situations, such as business planning, dealing with teenagers, picking a movie or cooking a meal, the process would be more **deliberate**.

BROCCOLI

I was on my usual pilgrimage to make my weekly donation to the local hardware store, when I stopped outside the front entrance to enjoy a charity's sausage sizzle. As I savoured the delights of a cheap sausage wrapped in a cheap slice of bread with cheap sauce and onions, I watched a young couple approach with a youngster over one shoulder and a child's bag over the other. I smiled at the thought that they were at the beginning of their life of future pilgrimages – a tradition passed down through the generations.

The child was obviously grumpy and not entirely ready to make the pilgrimage an enjoyable weekly event. This was WIKID POWER on the child's part – learned behavior is *knowledge, intelligence* and *wisdom*. To cry to get what they want would be *power*, and if successful, *superiority*.

I expected the parents would have a few tricks up their sleeves from their own WIKID POWER experiences and *knowledge*, especially since their frontal lobes were a tad more developed than their child's. To test my theory, I observed and waited for the blackmail device, often a lolly, to be produced and for the child to stop complaining. I watched as the parent looked only a tad miffed and dove into the bag. "Here comes the lolly!" I thought with a smile.

Out of the bag was produced a plastic Tupperware container. The lid was taken off and out came the blackmailing distraction: broccoli!

What? In my experience, I doubt I could have ever blackmailed my children to behave with an offer of a floret of broccoli.

The child was not tempted and remained defiant and undaunted. Hardly a surprise to me, but evidently a surprise to its parent. Back into the bag and another container was produced. "That's more like it," I thought "Why didn't you go for the lolly first?" Off came the lid and out of it was picked out a nice shiny red piece of capsicum. I choked on my sausage sizzle. I had not yet known a toddler to ever go anywhere near capsicum. The child took one look at the peace offering and with an indifferent look of disdain, turned its head and went quiet. With simultaneous surprise, the parent couldn't seem to fathom that the child turned down the capsicum, and I couldn't believe the child went quiet!

That morning, all three parties to that incident went through parts of the WIKID POWER process.

- We all cycled through the WIKID POWER process and gained much *knowledge* and *intelligence*.
- The parent and child both experienced *power* in influencing the situation.
- Only the parent experienced *superiority* because the child went quiet – not the way expected.
- The observation of how that *superiority* was achieved gave all three of us new *knowledge that will undoubtedly be used in future decisions*.

These are only a few quick looks at how WIKID POWER played its part in this situation. I'm sure you can find it in other areas of the story as you look at it from varying perspectives.

TEENAGERS

I love being around teenagers and there always seems to be a teenager or two, or more, hanging around my home. Their energy and enthusiasm is exhilarating. Their quaint naivety is cute as they learn what we consider, as more experienced adults, basic *knowledge* and skills. Often, this learning process is slower than desired.

It is a constant source of incredulity to observe what appears to be a common teenage perspective on life. At first, I thought that maybe it was purely parenting that had let the children down. To test this reasoned *intelligence*, I sought out other parents' observations, *knowledge, wisdom* and experience. With universal sighs of frustration, it appears most parents can finish the sentences of other parents of teenagers. The overwhelmingly common *intelligence* about teenagers from parents is that some haven't yet gone through the WIKID POWER process to learn that they are no longer the centre of attention where parents do everything for them.

Further, they may only learn a parent's perspective through their own personal experience when they become a parent rather than from hearing a parent's *wise* opinions.

Some *knowledge* can only be gained in certain ways!

Conversely, teenagers have their own perspective: "My parents don't know anything! I'm much more *knowledgeable* and *intelligent* than them. My decisions are *wise* ones."

No doubt the teenagers and their parents both go through the WIKID POWER process. Each conclude with varying degrees of *power* and *superiority*! A more experienced mind might conclude that:
- Teenagers don't go through the cycling of WIKID POWER as often as they should to reach *wise* decisions.
- Parents don't go through the cycling of WIKID POWER as often as they should to reach *superior* influence.

Teenagers are still only cycling through a few iterations of the WIKID POWER process because they don't have enough *knowledge* based on experience, simply because they have yet to experience much of the world. Without a broad base of experiential *knowledge*, their decisions are not as *wise* as parents often desire. Often, their *knowledge* has not yet been updated for changing circumstances, such as parents no longer should be responsible to clean their room. Sadly, as teenagers increasingly revert to their bedrooms and portable social technology, they are not taking advantage of the vast opportunities that have existed for thousands of years, where interacting and communicating with parents helps them to learn from others' mistakes and helps them make *wiser* decisions! Since success is where preparation meets opportunity, by not preparing and not taking up the opportunities, success is sometimes difficult for teenagers to obtain.

Similarly, parents are not cycling through enough iterations of the WIKID POWER process because we persist with an inadequate *knowledge* of the frontal lobe and what to expect from teenagers. Some parental *knowledge* still may not have been updated as their children matured, such as children listen to their parents, a behavior more likely to be attributed to pre-teens.

The more parents and teenagers work their way through the WIKID POWER process, the better the relationships will be. Perspective, cycling and being manoeuvrable are the keys to success in the relationship between teenagers and parents.

STOCK MARKET SCAMS

When I studied success, I looked at various methods for wealth generation. One of the methods that intrigued me was trading on the stock market. As a student of mathematics and probabilities, and a devotee of problem solving techniques, I was eager to see if a *knowledge* of mathematics could assist success. Since the outcomes are easy to measure through the prices traded, it would be relatively easy to prove or disprove.

Over quite a few years, I looked at various methods and paper-traded two specific methods for a year each. During that time, I followed their rules carefully. The results were disappointing, especially given the enormous effort I had put in. My conclusion was not new: there are many more influences, than simply trends, that are unknown to the market as the price is set, such as confidential work within companies, unexpected announcements and Board and Executive performance.

Whilst insider trading is illegal, it would be quite unrealistic to think that it doesn't happen. Of quite fanciful intrigue to me were two fictional stories, the first was the film *Trading Places* with Eddie Murphy and Dan Aykroyd, where a particular scene showed that the stock market was manipulated by heavy trading of orange concentrate in anticipation of an impending announcement about the orange crop harvest predictions. When the announcement was made, many discovered they had been tricked into buying it too high and started selling in a frenzy that financially ruined two characters in the story. The second was the first novel *Not a Penny More, Not a Penny Less* by best-selling author and politician Jeffrey Archer, that amply demonstrated how to manipulate the market for gain.

Whilst both examples were in the times where stock markets traded in pits, these days this rarely happens and the digital technology of today, including the ever-pervasive and instantaneous Internet, has made such situations with the stock market difficult to replicate – although not impossible. New ways to manipulate the market are always being investigated. Unethical people are always working on innovations to financially manipulate situations for gain. The use of technology offers many opportunities not previously available.

Manipulation of a stock market is a perfect example of the WIKID POWER transformation all the way through to *power* and *superiority* in a particular situation and environment.

To many people, they don't want to believe stock market scams exist for two reasons:

1. they have stock and don't want to believe they are potentially vulnerable, and
2. they don't have personal experience or *knowledge* of it and hence, it is outside their perspective.

Such denial is an example of cognitive bias.

Some prefer to stop the WIKID POWER process so that they don't have to conclude the inevitable *wisdom*. Likewise, some people will also consider that world domination is unrealistic.

WORLD DOMINATION

In days gone by, it was easy to propagate propaganda. The reason for propaganda was to give an impression of a situation that was not reality, to control what people thought.

There are many examples throughout history where propaganda has been used to great effect during times of war and in politics. There are also many examples where commercial propaganda is disseminated through marketing, and again, there are examples of propaganda in dating where people try to impress a potential partner with flattering or fanciful talk of themselves. Propaganda is an application of WIKID POWER and is used as a tool of those seeking domination of people, a population or the world.

Politics

Success in public elections requires, in most cases, the majority of people to vote for you. As you step through life and see more elections, you will notice that the media can influence public perception simply by emphasizing various issues and de-emphasizing others. The public sees a version that the media portrays and votes according to what they *know* through the media. The people that own various media outlets understand the influence that they have to exercise *power*. Some may resist the temptation, others may not. The more media that any individual entity acquires, the more control they might wield, and potentially exercise. Global media entities may exercise influence on a much larger scale and have the potential for some domination of global thought. A form of world domination is possible through the judicious use of *information*.

Popularity and Social Media

Popularity has long been a method used to gain influence and control. In many small elections, such as at school, it is generally the more popular people who are elected. As the years progress, a similar story repeats. The use of social media helps to leverage popularity and the potential for domination.

I saw this happen at a charity's election of the Board of Directors. A popular and successful fundraiser nominated to be elected, but had little experience. That person used their social media following to easily swamp the election that previously only had a modest number of voters attend. Their election forced out a Director who had turned the flailing charity around, helped it grow significantly over several years and was spearheading strategies to succeed under new challenges. Despite an indisputable passion and heart of gold, the new director's inexperience was quickly felt and the charity's progress was impacted. As one lamenting person told me, "They elected who they wanted, but not who they needed."

Popularity can easily be used to dominate and control. Social media offers opportunities for that to happen easier and faster. Testament to the use of social media in elections on a far grander scale was Barack Obama's impressive social media campaign to be elected the President of the United States of America. His use of social media greatly impacted voter attendance, as well as the number of votes he received. It was an "aha" moment for many politicians who have since undertaken social media campaigns on top of their traditional door to door visits and shopping centre appearances.

One of the impacts of social media is that popularity is self-feeding: the more likes and shares given, the more they generate. If one has a strong following, this is leveraged even further as the likes and shares are instantly generated rather than organically grown. With social media platforms highlighting trending profiles and posts, this can be promoted beyond the followers and instead to the entire platform's users. Popularity generates more popularity.

Social media offers many efficiencies for those seeking domination, including the ability to reach a greater number of people using only a small amount of resources. Staying abreast of Internet technologies and trends is vital for domination.

Internet Monitoring

Cookies have long been used on the Internet to allow *data* to be stored on an individual's computer and accessed by programs when a website is visited or re-visited. The primary aim is to enhance the user experience through a memory, via cookies, of preferences for each site. Cookies may also be used to deliver targeted messages. For instance, if a cookie collects your age, gender, location and marital status, a website that accesses the *data* in that cookie may deliver targeted advertisements such as for singles events in your location. The use of cookies can, therefore, be used to help dominate a market.

Now consider a concept proposed by best-selling author of *The Da Vinci Code*, Dan Brown. In one of his other books, *Digital Fortress*, he proposes a situation where all Internet transactions are monitored by a secret supercomputer in one of the USA's intelligence agencies. Should such a capability be plausible, and this is increasingly believable as technology capabilities explode, then it is also plausible that such *information* could be used against an entity to control them – Information Warfare. The smaller the entity, the easier to control through the use of *information*. The larger the entity or entities, the more effort that will be required.

As well as propaganda and marketing, blackmail is another form of control and domination through the use of *information*. The increasing amount of personal *information* shared via the Internet offers unscrupulous people enormous opportunities for control via blackmail and this is already being witnessed. I'm sure you can think of other examples.

Some people claim that, in recent decades, there have been some small countries that had sustained Information Warfare attacks and been brought to their knees, only being saved by an entity that thereafter wields an element of control.

If domination of entities through the use of *information* is a reality, the question becomes one of scale – how much influence and domination is possible? Is it hard to imagine a political figure that wants world domination? We would like to think that sort of personality only lives in the past, a time of world wars many decades ago or conquering forces many centuries ago. However, as we look at history since then, we can see that that sort of personality still exists. As I write this, the news is full of stories of two separate powers attempting to expand their reach and to ultimately take over the world, or large parts of it.

As you might well imagine, when I was in Army Headquarters and working on WIKID POWER, I also quickly became known as the go-to person on Information Warfare (IW). WIKID POWER and IW lay frameworks to guide the control of an environment – whether it be through propaganda, marketing, blackmail or whatever. The WIKID POWER framework I developed for IW builds on the WIKID POWER transformation in decision-making and is also applicable in everyday life as much as it is in a military sense. Although I have not covered the WIKID POWER IW framework in this book, if you study examples of control, you should be able to map them to both of my WIKID POWER frameworks to see how control can be planned.

World domination takes careful planning.

What is the WIKID Value?

You've gone through the WIKID POWER process and transformations. You may even be recognizing it everywhere and saying to yourself, "That's WIKID POWER!"

The value is clear. Yet, like the TV salesman I feel compelled to exclaim "But wait! There's more!" Why did Defence authorities want to classify WIKID POWER beyond TOP SECRET? What did they really want to have exclusively, and to not let anyone else have?

SPIES AND THIEVES

There is a difference between the motivations and goals of spies and thieves. Thieves want things; spies want *information*.

Sometimes, a spy may need to become a thief to get the *information* they need, but in the end, spies primarily seek *information* and *knowledge*, which will be converted into *intelligence* and *wisdom* to gain *power* and *superiority*.

Let me tell you four stories.

National Intelligence

A subordinate of mine in Army Headquarters told me he was being transferred to an intelligence agency. He was a pleasant and clever young chap with a physical twitch. I was sorry to see him go, especially as he left so suddenly and we had more work to do! I thought nothing more of it until a short while later, when I was approached by someone I knew. The conversation was casual. And just as casually, I was asked to join a particular intelligence agency. Looking over my shoulder – more than I already do – was not something I desired. Also, I preferred to be able to tell people honestly what I did rather than say I was a greeting card salesman – the fictional job of the fictional Maxwell Smart, Agent 86, from one of my favorite TV shows of the late 1960's, *Get Smart*.

The offer was politely rejected.

International Incident

Around this time, I was tasked as the Contingent Commander for a three-nation international exchange. It involved 320 Army personnel from Australia, New Zealand and the United Kingdom, with 160 British personnel exchanged with 120 Aussies and 40 Kiwis.

After sorting out the Brits in Sydney, I flew the Kiwis and Aussies in a westerly direction to the other side of the world. We departed from the very end of the international airport terminal and it was weird to personally make the announcement over the terminal speaker system for flight RR001, as I had command of a RAF Tristar air-to-air refueller. It was noisy and cold as we sat in the weight- and insulation-reduced fuselage above the fuel tank, which occupied the lower half of the aircraft. Consequently, I was pleased for every distraction on the long, tedious flight and delighted when breakfast was delivered by the cabin staff. After what seemed an eternity, but in reality was only about five or so hours, the next meal arrived. What? Breakfast again? They must have made a mistake. I asked the crew and they confirmed that the time zone in the part of the world we were flying over was still morning – that mandated breakfast. We had three breakfasts in a row as we chased the sun in a westerly direction.

After stopping in Europe to drop off some personnel who were to be stationed there, we continued onto a military airport near London (This later caused me a problem as I tried to take a quick trip to Paris one weekend. Since my green passport hadn't been stamped on arrival, authorities were unclear whether I had actually arrived in the UK. It was difficult to ignore the fact that I was actually standing on UK soil).

My staff and I were headquartered in Australia House on The Strand, collocated with the Australian High Commission and right opposite the church of St Clement Danes; the church referred to in the nursery rhyme *Oranges and Lemons, the Bells of St Clement's*, and also where one of my relatives, Air Marshall Lord Tedder, Deputy

Supreme Commander to Eisenhower in WWII, is commemorated. Australia House is magnificent in architecture and has a most amazing hall, with opulent marble and chandeliers. It is often requested to be used for films and functions. One interesting and little-known piece of history involves its security, since it once was the stronghold for Australia's gold bullion reserves.

Our tiny office was at the very top of the building, on the southeast side facing The Strand, and had a small oval window. Access to the building was via a special security entrance for staff at street level below. Access to the floor was via a security device issued only to the staff authorized to visit that floor. Access to the office required a third security check – a security key and I had the only one.

One morning, I arrived at the office and found the door had been forced open and material had been sought out and taken. Someone had breached three levels of security in a very secure building to steal a computer, which had sensitive *information*.

Australian, British and international authorities investigated immediately while we made alternate arrangements to look after our personnel, who were by now in over 20 countries.

The event remained a mystery and we never found out what really happened.

Home Infiltration

When I was working in G building, I lived in a modest house ten minutes' walk from the military compound. The house was built shortly after WWII and was a standard three-bedroom house, but had an extension which I had converted into a self-contained flat. For a bit of extra money, the flat was rented out. The first (and only) tenant was quick to apply and take up the offer. The timing was perfect. I had finished and launched the Army Information Management Manual, trained others in the use of the GDSS, was giving high level presentations about WIKID POWER, and was about to head up a three-nation exchange program where I would be based in London's Australia House, co-located with the High Commission.

Immediately after the tenant moved in, the phone started clicking after each call was answered. Sometimes, I could hear a click after the phone call ended. Funny noises were heard on the line. There was no phone line in the self-contained flat. The clicks and noises weren't there before the tenant moved in. I thought nothing of it other than coincidence.

After my return from London, the tenant moved out. I was intrigued to later discover that they worked for one of our intelligence organizations.

Commercial Enterprise

Shortly after leaving the Army, I was approached yet again. This time, it was to head up a joint venture involving the military and industry. The role was to develop advanced military technologies and capabilities. This was right up my alley and I was excited. Clearances had already been approved and I was taken on a drive for a tour of the extensive facility I would have. The tour was incredible. I had never seen anything like it. This was a serious complex for some serious work. Its TEMPEST electromagnetic security safeguards were impressive to say the least. It's a facility nobody notices and has so many unusual features, it would send the conspiracy theorists into a frenzy. One particular room had quite extraordinary dimensions, and when I humorously mentioned a possible use, my guides went ashen-faced and silent. We finished the tour and returned.

After that, I heard nothing for a short while. Unusual things started happening. I was no longer available for the role.

THE WIKID PUNCH LINE

It is clear to me, from my own experiences and other sources, that there are some people who will go to extraordinary lengths to achieve *superiority*. Whatever situation or environment you're in, whether in the home, business, sport, pastime or social scene, you will need to work out how to stay in control of your world and what *superiority* you need.

You'll need to consider who and what will be standing in your way, and what you need to overcome others. You'll go through the WIKID POWER model yourself, working out what extra *information* you need to *know* to get the required *intelligence* and make *wise* decisions about what you need to do to succeed and gain control. Then you need to have the courage to take the next step – taking action to exercise *power* and work towards *superiority*. If you don't do it, there will be others who will, and they will reign *superior* rather than you.

Read what you like into the stories. The main thing is to use them as examples to help you better understand and use WIKID POWER for your own *superiority*.

WIKID POWER is about transforming *data* and *information* into *knowledge, intelligence, wisdom* and *power*.

Through *Information Warfare*, we primarily protect, and sometimes attack, to convert *Information Power* into *Information*

Superiority in the *Information Environment*. Mastery of WIKID POWER is essential for Information Warfare and *superiority*.

Planning is essential for *Information Superiority* and sometimes, unusual or innovative methods may be considered to be needed. Reconnaissance, stealing, spying, research and simply asking questions help to collect the *information* we need for *superiority*.

THREE COMMON TRIP-UPS

Having observed the use of WIKID POWER for many years now, I have identified the three areas where people most frequently stumble and trip in the process.
1. They have failed to understand their core desires, goals and criteria for success and hence fail in the collection of useful *data*.
2. When they have useful *knowledge*, they fail to wonder how to use it or how it relates to other *knowledge*. They don't incorporate other relevant bits of *knowledge* and hence, they fail to produce useful *intelligence* and fail to gain *superiority*. This allows others to gain *superiority* over them.
3. Should they produce *wise* decisions, many fail to take action in a timely manner, or at all, often allowing others to take the initiative and gain *superiority* instead of them.

MY THREE VITAL TIPS

My three top decision-making tips are:
1. Know your goal and your core desire.
2. Follow the WIKID POWER process through to *superiority*.
3. Exercise OODA loop decisiveness and know the consequences.

If you know what your goal is, then your WIKID POWER process will be highly targeted and more effective. If you don't fully work through the WIKID POWER process, including the tips for use, then the outcome may not be *superiority*. Yet, the impact of decisiveness can be the absolute clincher!

YOUR PERSONAL VALUE

Some of you would have read this book for personal development, and others may have had more professional reasons to pick up the book. Whilst you would have found some of the material easy to read and comprehend, there would have been places that were harder going. You may have even skipped over them thinking that they were not relevant to your circumstances. That's to be expected.

As your Reticular Activating System kicks in, you will notice WIKID POWER in action in all sorts of situations in everyday life and at work. You may even catch yourself saying "That's WIKID POWER!" As you gain experience with it, you'll get better at it.

What I hope you will also find is a desire to re-read the book from time to time. To pick up subtleties you may have missed so that you can better master WIKID POWER for your benefit. As you do, you will find gems that you may have missed earlier, just as watching a movie again helps you get a deeper insight into certain aspects as you observe things you didn't notice earlier. I have been dealing with WIKID POWER for quite some time now, and I am constantly surprised at the numerous "aha" moments I still experience as I go over various parts of it in different circumstances.

WIKID POWER is a transformation process that helps you succeed in controlling your situation. The WIKID POWER framework for IW (not covered in this book) provides a formalized structure for strengthening your *superiority*, whether personally (such as with virus protection) or professionally (in a competitive situation). Whilst you may not wish to call it Information Warfare, protection and defence against threats is still a form of warfare – and you're doing it every day.

I hope that I have given you food for thought and helped you realize a method for making more influential decisions on your search for success. My wish for you is that you find yourself closer to your desires and goals by applying WIKID POWER.

Through WIKID POWER, may you develop the hindsight to appreciate where you've been, insight to understand where you are, and foresight to reach where you are going.

Join the community of superior decision-makers at
WIKIDPOWER.com
and register as someone who has read the book!

ABOUT THE AUTHOR

Ian was born in Sydney, Australia and joined the Army immediately following school. After an enjoyable and rewarding time as an Officer in Artillery and training Recruits and Officer Cadets, he was posted to Army Headquarters and was responsible for Army's software. It was here that Ian first worked on WIKID POWER whilst instigating Army's first Information Management policy and plans manual. During the same time, he also instigated Army's Group Decision Support System and in essence became an internal adviser using it to facilitate meetings to develop budgets, restructures, plans and other decisions, as well as training others to use it.

After 20 years in the Army, Ian retired to set up his own consulting firm in Canberra and was sought out to continue his decision facilitation fascination.

Ian moved to Brisbane and continued advising businesses and CEOs whilst also continuing volunteer work in the nonprofit sector. He has been honoured as Community Leader of the Year for South East Queensland in the Australian Leadership Excellence Awards (ALEAs).

He has settled with his partner and since all the children are now adults, Ian spends his time researching, authoring, speaking, advising, helping social enterprises and charities, and doing household chores.

www.ingramcontent.com/pod-product-compliance
Lightning Source LLC
Chambersburg PA
CBHW060340170426
43202CB00014B/2836